THE CHEAP BASTARD'S® GUIDE

Washington, D.C.

Secrets of Living the Good Life—**For Free!**

Rob **Grader**

travel

Guilford, Connecticut
An imprint of Globe Pequot Press

All the information in this guidebook is subject to change. We recommend that you call ahead to obtain current information before traveling.

Text design by Sheryl P. Kober

ISBN: 978-0-7627-5336-9

Printed in the United States of America

10 9 8 7 6 5 4 3 2 1

For Roscoe and Henry,
the very proof that the best things in life are free.

CONTENTS

Section 3: Exploring D.C.

Appendices

ACKNOWLEDGMENTS

This Cheap Bastard is rich in friends and family members who haven't been stingy with their helpful advice, suggestions, and patience while I worked on this book. With empty pockets and a full heart, I want to acknowledge some of the people who have given me their 2 cents along the way. First and foremost, thanks to Karen and Roscoe for your endless patience and help. You can come down to the basement now. Thanks to my Mom and Dad, Bernice and Jack, for making me the Cheap Bastard that I am; to my in-laws Elaine Raksis and Maxine "Ya Ya" Klane, who are not Cheap Bastards, but I am working on them; and to the rest of my family who are always generous with their support: the Graders—Scott, Trish, Lulu, Stu, Ellen, Jessica, Michelle, Jeff, Lisa, Emily, Sally, and Jonas; and the Raksises—Gary, Joe, and Marybeth Budd.

I owe a debt of gratitude to the many friends, associates, and others I met while researching this tome. In particular, thanks to Steve Harper for always being free to talk and Suzi Takahashi for free advice. Thanks to Amy Lyons at Globe Pequot Press and to the many people who have made so many useful suggestions: Paul Mermelstein; Jenny Kelty; Angela Kondo; Suzie, Bruce and Michael Shulman; Edith "Khayke" Hoffman; Scott Harrison; Sharon Harrison; Lorna V. Kivlehan; Donna M. Bohanon; Harrison M. Wadsworth IV; Senthil Sankaran; Mary Szegda; and Erin Dowdy. From the bottom of my empty piggy bank, I thank you all.

A Note about the Listings:

The listings in this book are spread throughout the Washington, D.C., region, including the nearby counties in Maryland and Virginia. For clarity, any listings located outside D.C. proper include the city and state and those within The District do not.

Land of the Free

A tour guide was showing a tourist around Washington, D.C. The guide pointed out the place where George Washington supposedly threw a dollar across the Potomac River.

"That's impossible," said the tourist. "No one could throw a coin that far!"

"You have to remember," answered the guide. "A dollar went a lot farther in those days."

Now I understand. Growing up in New York, I used to wonder why every year my parents packed my three brothers and me into the car for a trip to Washington, D.C. Were they incredibly patriotic and hoping to instill in us a love of country, a respect for its history, government, and diverse population? Was it to inspire us to stand for what we believe in as our founding fathers did, to fight for the freedom of all people as Abraham Lincoln did, to selflessly serve our country as the men and women buried at Arlington Cemetery did? Naaah, it was just the cheapest vacation they could find. Now that I have grown into a Cheap Bastard with a family of my own, I understand the appeal. And while a lot has changed since I was a kid, D.C. is still the place to be for freebies-a-plenty. Whether you live here or are visiting, the amount of free stuff available is simply astonishing.

On our family vacation, we toured the Capitol, sat in on the Supreme Court, visited the top of the Washington Monument and spent time in the Air and Space Museum. We watched money being made at the Bureau of Printing and Engraving, posed for pictures in front of the Iwo Jima Memorial, and watched the Changing of the Guard at Arlington National Cemetery. We thought we had exhausted all the free possibilities. And while the Smithsonian is fantastic, the monuments are evocative, and the government buildings are awe-inspiring, they are just the tip of the free iceberg.

The Cheap Bastard's Guide is your handbook to everything free in D.C., from the well tread upon to the little known experiences, hidden perks, and secret strategies for living the good life for free. This book will take you to places you didn't know existed, and give you the chance to do things you didn't think you could afford to do. That is the mission of The Cheap Bastard, to offer you a chance at something more valuable than money: a memory, an experience, a story. And of course the chance to save a boatload of cash ain't such a bad thing either.

Ever wanted to learn how to tango? Why not take lessons at the Argentinean Embassy? Need to stay at work till the wee hours? Forget about laying out $50 for a taxi. The Cheap Bastard can get you a free ride home. You'd love to spend the summer enjoying the concerts at Wolf Trap but just can't swing the ticket prices? No sweat. The Cheap Bastard can show you how to slip into every show of the season for free. And it's all legal.

The listings in this book can be split into two categories: Free and Ridiculously Cheap, with the vast majority of the listings being free. Free doesn't mean "Buy One, Get One Free," "First Month Free," "Mention the Cheap Bastard and get in for half-price," or any other scheme that is ultimately about getting cash out of your wallet.

What kinds of free listings will you find in this book? Free-free and Free-with-a-catch. Want to learn a foreign language? Check out the Global Language Network at George Washington University for free classes in everything from Arabic to Urdu, no strings attached. Free with a catch generally means you will need to spend some time or effort to get that something for free. For example, you can see a show at almost any theater in the D.C. area for free by being a volunteer usher. Show up an hour early, help seat the paying customers, and watch the show for nothing. I have tried to clearly explain any catch you may need to know about, by including the category *The Catch* wherever necessary.

Ridiculously Cheap listings are those for which, yes, you will have to lay out some money. Still, the cost is so minimal that when you're asked to pay, you do it quickly for fear that it's a mistake.

Cheap Bastard is a proud term and refers to someone who enjoys the thrill of the hunt, not someone who is stingy or denies himself or anyone else simply because it costs something. Most importantly, a Cheap Bastard is not out to beat another person out of a few cents; he or she is out to beat the system.

This book is intended for visitors and locals alike: from a family from Ohio trying to make the most of a week in D.C. without breaking the bank to European backpackers banking on the Euro having a better exchange rate to born and bred Washingtonians who need to stretch that federal paycheck a little farther to Capitol Hill interns trying to make ends meet to college students who need to figure out how to make that student loan last all year to those for whom money is not a worry.

All the information in this guide is accurate as of press time, but contrary to popular belief, things do change quickly in Washington, so I have included as much contact information as possible. Always call ahead, check Web sites or stop by a venue to make sure all the information in this book is still accurate. If you have any thoughts, comments, corrections, or suggestions for future volumes, please contact me via www.thecheapbastard.com or e-mail at thecheapbastard@gmail.com.

SECTION 1:

Entertainment in Washington, D.C.

THEATER:
FREE SPEECH

"Of all men, physicians and playwrights alone possess the rare priviledge of charging money for the pain they inflict on us."

—SANTIAGO RAMON Y CAJAL

You may think the only drama going on in Washington is between the Democrats and the Republicans, but you would be wrong. Washington has quite a vibrant theater scene that includes touring productions of Broadway shows, off Broadway productions, originals, cutting-edge performances, classics, and theater for young audiences—and just about all of it can be had for a song.

VOLUNTEER USHERING

When you walk into a theater to see a show, some kindly person takes your ticket and shows you to your seat. Often you find these folks are just so happy to be doing this job. Ever wonder why? Well, they are just there for that night to see the show like you. The only difference is they haven't paid a red cent to get in. Yes, they are volunteer ushers, and you can find them at almost every theater in D.C. Considering the ticket price of shows (from $15 to $75) volunteer ushers get "paid" very well.

Ushers get to watch from seats that remain empty as the show is about to start. There are almost always good seats; many times they are the best seats in the house for you to fill (even if the show is officially sold-out). On the very rare occasion that there are absolutely no seats available they may set up some chairs, or in some extremely rare instances they may ask you to sit in the aisles. Occasionally you need to stay a couple of minutes after the show to help pick up stray programs. It is pretty darn simple. Why do theaters do this? Economics. It is cheaper to let you in for nothing than to hire a full-time ushering staff. You can even bring a friend. Most theaters need at least two ushers per show (some as many as 26) and are usually happy to let you reserve more than one slot. Talk about your cheap dates!

It is simple to join the usher ranks. Each theater has its own system that generally works one of two ways that I call "freelance" or "fully committed."

The freelance version: All that is involved is making a reservation a week or two in advance and showing up an hour before the curtain rises. The house manager will give you a quick run-down on the seating plan (*warning:* you do need to be able to count to 12—sometimes even backwards—to understand this). Your job is to help seat the paying folks and enjoy the show. The freelance version is the way it works at many of the small- to medium-sized theaters.

Pick a Price, Any Price!

Just about every theater in D.C. offers some **Pay-What-You-Can (PWYC)** performances, discounted rush tickets for the day or week of the performance and great discounts for younger theatergoers. PWYC performances often take place during the previews of the shows but can also take place during the run. Following is a list of many of the discounts offered at D.C. theaters. If a theater you are interested in is not on the list, call or check its Web site as it will probably have a PWYC performance or some other discount available at some point during the run. The take-home message—never pay full price!

Arena Stage: Offers half-priced tickets at the theater the day of the show. Also, if you are under 30, you can snag $10 tickets every Monday for that week's performances.

Folger Theater: Sells half-priced tickets at the box office one hour before showtime.

Ford's Theatre: $10 tickets for selected previews. Check its Web site for specific dates.

Gala Hispanic Theater: Sells $18 rush tickets starting an hour and a half before showtime.

Journeymen Theater: Every Wednesday is PWYC.

Kennedy Center: Standing room tickets are available for sold-out shows, check prices at box office. The Attend program offers heavily discounted tickets to anyone 17 to 25. Register at www.kennedy-center.org/tickets/attend.

Mead Theatre Lab at Flashpoint: The first two or three previews are always PWYC.

Metro State: The first preview of every production is always PWYC ($10 is suggested).

The fully committed version: To join the corps of volunteer ushers at some of the larger theaters (Arena, Ford's, Signature, etc.) you need to commit to ushering at least once for each production of the season. They may ask you to adhere to a set schedule throughout the season (for instance, you would always usher the first Thursday night performances of the run). You

Rep Stage: All Wednesday evening performances are PWYC.

Rorschack Theater: First three previews of every production are PWYC.

Round House Theatre: The first preview of every show on the main stage is PWYC; anyone 25 or under can get $25 tickets for any production.

Olney Theatre: $10 student tickets are available the day of the show and a PWYC performance on the Tuesday during previews for most shows.

Shakespeare Theater Company: $10 standing-room tickets are available one hour before curtain for sold-out shows. Also, anyone 35 or under can try for $10 tickets on Tuesday for that week's performances.

Signature Theatre: $30 rush tickets are available one hour before all performances.

Spooky Action Theater: The first three or four previews are PWYC.

Studio Theatre: $30 rush tickets are available a half hour before curtain.

Synetic Theatre: The last preview before opening night is PWYC.

Theater Alliance: The first one or two previews are PWYC.

Theater J: The first two previews are PWYC. Sunday nights are half-priced.

Washington Stage Guild: All previews are PWYC.

Woolly Mammoth: Ten $15 "Stampede" tickets are sold two hours before most performances. The first two performances of most shows are PWYC and patrons 25 or under can buy $15 tickets to the production of their choice.

may be required to go through an orientation early in the season to learn the theater's ushering protocol. Just as with freelance ushering, on the day of the performance show up early, help seat the suckers . . . err, I mean paying folks, and then enjoy the show.

Adventure Theatre

Glen Echo Park
7300 MacArthur Blvd. (Oxford Road at MacArthur Boulevard)
Glen Echo, MD
(301) 634-2270
www.adventuretheatre.org
Ushers per performance: 2 to 3

A delightful children's theater company, Adventure produces a fun season of shows that are generally targeted for kids from age three to early teens. They use volunteer ushers as young as 12 or 13. It is pretty easy to sign up for a performance; just call and tell them when you want to come! They also have a Pay-What-You-Can performance on the Thursday before a show opens. A $5 donation is suggested.

Arena Stage

Permanent Address (under construction)
1101 Sixth St., SW (at Maine Avenue)
Temporary spaces:
Crystal City 1800 S. Bell St. (at 20th St.), Arlington, VA
Lincoln Theater 1215 U St., NW (at 14th St.)
(202) 488-3300
usher@arenastage.org
www.arena-stage.org
Ushers per performance: 26

Arena Stage is an elder statesmen among American regional theaters. For more than 50 years it has been producing plays and musicals that attract some of the most talented actors, directors, and playwrights from across the county. Over the years they have developed a number of plays that have gone on to long runs in New York or internationally. Arena is in the midst of expanding its permanent home on 6th St. and in the interim has been staging its performances at other venues in the area.

I have to tell you: it can be pretty competitive to nab a spot as an usher here. The first thing to do is sign up for the ushering email list on the ushering page of its Web site. Once you get an application to sign-up for a season of ushering (they are sent out over the summer) send it in *immediately*. Ushers are required to make a full-season commitment to work a specific day for each production throughout the season, and you are required to attend an orientation in September.

Don't fret if you don't make the elite ushering list. Keep an eye on the theater's blog for an invitation to an open-dress rehearsal held the night before the first preview of every show. There are even some refreshments! Also, there are a couple of discounted ticket options: for anyone under 30, every Monday there are $10 tickets available for the coming week's performances. Finally, if they are available, anyone can pick up half-priced tickets at the box office the night of the show.

Atlas Performing Arts Center
1333 H St., NE (between 13th and 14th Sts.)
(202) 399-7993, ext 2
info@atlasarts.org
www.atlasarts.org
Ushers per performance: 2 to 8 (depending on the evening)

Atlas is a gold mine of theater, music, and dance performances. This community-based arts center has dubbed itself "the people's Kennedy Center." Atlas has five separate venues and is home to three theater companies: **Catalyst Theater, The Washington Savoyards,** and **the African Continuum Theatre Company.** Because the Atlas has so many performances going on at one time, there is no guarantee you will get to see the show of your choice on the night you volunteer, but you will get a voucher to come back to see any other performance at the theater. To volunteer, email or call the box office.

The American Century Theater
2700 South Lang St. (at 28th St. S)
Arlington, VA
(703) 998-4555
www.americancentury.org
Ushers per performance: 2

American Century is a small company specializing in producing twentieth-century American plays that include everything from works by Eugene O'Neill to Terrence McNally. To usher, send an email a few weeks in advance. All Wednesday performances are Pay-What-You-Can.

The Bethesda Theatre

7719 Wisconsin Ave. (at Cheltenham Street)
Bethesda, MD
(301) 657-7827
ushers@bethesdatheatre.com
www.bethesdatheatre.com
Ushers per performance: 4 to 6

The Bethesda is out to make you smile. Every season the theater plays host to a series of lighthearted off-Broadway musicals, plays, and one-man shows touring the country. Past shows include *Forbidden Broadway, Menopause, The Musical,* and *Alter Boyz.* Send an email to find out more about the ushering program. If you are up for a double feature, usher on Friday or Saturday nights, when performances are followed by a late-night comedy improv show.

Dress the Part

While no special skills or training are needed to be a volunteer usher, a nice pair of black pants and a crisp white shirt are often required. Many theaters do ask you to look the role, although you are playing the part for only one evening. The dress codes vary from black and white (black pants and a white shirt) to all black, while some just ask you to look respectable. Be sure to ask what to wear when making reservations. Most theaters are flexible in these requirements, but some do take them very seriously and will not allow you to usher if you are not dressed properly.

Dance Place

3225 8th St., NE (at Kearny Street)
(202) 269-1600
www.danceplace.org
Ushers per performance: 4

Dance Place is considered one of the main hubs for dance in D.C. Every weekend it hosts performances of modern and African dances by companies from D.C. and elsewhere. Call to sign up for an ushering slot.

Folger Shakespeare Library

201 E. Capitol St., SE (at 2nd St.)
(202) 544-4600 (general number)
(202) 675-0391 (ushering)
(202) 544-7077 (box office)
Volunteer@folger.edu
www.folger.edu
Ushers per performance: 7 to 8

The Folger is the world's largest collection of Shakespeare materials and a treasure trove of free opportunities to get your fill of Will. It offers a season of wide-ranging performances that includes not only Shakespeare but also readings, lectures, music, and family performances. You can usher for any one of those shows or events. To sign up for a performance, send an email with your specific request or ask to be added to the ushering mailing list. The Folger has a pretty large ushering pool, so slots usually fill up far in advance, but you can always call to try for a last-minute opening. It also offers free tours of its exhibitions, historic theater and building, and (during the summer) garden. The tours happen Monday through Friday at 11 a.m. and 3 p.m. and Saturdays at 11 a.m. and 1 p.m. Finally, don't miss the annual celebration of Shakespeare's birthday each April. The raucous family celebration is free and includes performances, crafts, games, period musicians, magic shows, and, of course, cake for all!

Ford's Theatre

511 10th St., NW (between E and F Streets)
(202) 347-4833 (box office)
(202) 434-9522 (ushering)
volunteer@fords.org
www.fords.org
Ushers per performance: 15 to 20

On the evening of April 14, 1865, Ford's Theatre became the most infamous theater in the country with the assassination of Abraham Lincoln. Ford's has embraced its tragic history and is dedicated to keeping the ideals of leadership and humanity and the wisdom of Abraham Lincoln alive. The newly renovated theater presents a lineup of productions from and about Lincoln's time. It uses volunteer ushers for all performances; to reserve a slot, email or call with your request. It is usually possible to get an ushering slot a few days to a week in advance.

The theater puts together other less-formal readings and performances that are free as well. Check out the Web site for a schedule of those events. You can also take a free tour of the historic theater, museum, and the Petersen House across the street where Lincoln was taken after he was shot. The tours are free but they do require a ticket for timed entrances. Line up at the box office for same-day tickets starting at 8:30 a.m. Tickets are given out on a first-come, first-served basis. You can reserve advanced tickets, but they charge you a few bucks for that.

All the World's a Cheap Bastard!

On one night every year, Cheap Bastards far and wide gather together to join in on a one-of-a-kind event that seems too good to be true. The event **Free Night of Theater** takes place in mid-October every year and happens in cities across the country, including D.C. and Baltimore. On this night, theaters throw open their doors for folks to attend any of the area's major theaters (Arena Stage, Bethesda Theater, Folger Theater, Roundhouse, Shakespeare Theater, Woolly Mammoth, and many others) completely free of charge. Why do they do this? Simple: they want to turn on more people to the joy of a night at the theater, and there is nothing like making it free to bring in the throngs! There are a limited number of free tickets available for each show, and they go fast. Reservations are only accepted online, and the tickets go "on sale" about two weeks prior to the event. For more information, go to www.freenightoftheater.net or www.lowt.org/fnot /fnothome.

Gala Hispanic Theatre
3333 14th St., NW (at Park Road)
(202) 234-7174
info@galatheatre.org
www.galatheatre.org
Ushers per performance: 5

This "theater with a different accent" presents classical and contemporary plays in Spanish and English as well as a full schedule of dance and musical performances. Volunteer ushers are used for all performances; call or email as late as the day of the performance, and you may be able to grab a spot. Of course, if you can contact the theater a week or so in advance, you are almost sure to get in on the day you want. You can also pick up $18 rush tickets starting an hour and a half before showtime. If you feel like getting down and dirty, you can pitch in with some tech work during the production. Anyone who helps out for five hours earns a free ticket to the show. Sign up for the theater's mailing list for more discount offers.

In The Series
1835 14th St., NW (at T Street)
(202) 204-7769
www.inseries.org
Ushers per performance: 3

This unique company produces an eclectic season of shows that include opera, cabaret, and musical theater as well as Latino programs and one Mozart production every year. To usher, call a week or two before the day you would like to attend.

Journeymen Theater
Church Street Theater
1742 Church St., NW (between 17th and 18th and Q & P Streets)
(202) 669-7229
www.journeymentheater.org
Ushers per performance: 2 to 4

The Journeymen produces thought-provoking and entertaining shows that in some, not-always-obvious ways go along with its faith-based mission. The often-surprising mix of plays ranges from classics by Molière and Gogol to new plays by up-and-coming writers and theater artists. To reserve an ushering spot, call the office a few days prior. Journeyman also has a Pay-What-You-Can performance every Wednesday. You can attend a series of free readings of new plays on the morning of the second Saturday of every month. Check its Web site for location and details.

Olney Theatre Center

2001 Olney Sandy Spring Rd. (between Route 108 and Dr. Bird Road)
Olney, MD
(301) 924-4485 ext 250 (ushering hotline)
www.olneytheatre.org
Ushers per performance: 6 to 15 (depending on venue)

Every year Olney produces a jam-packed season of eight or more productions of twentieth-century American classics, musicals, new plays, and area
premieres. To join the ushering corps, you have to commit to usher at every
show throughout the season. To apply, call the ushering hotline. The theater
offers $10 student rush tickets available on the night of the performance
and a Pay-What-You-Can performance for most shows on the Tuesday performance during previews. Every summer Olney also presents a free Shakespeare production.

Rep Stage

10901 Little Patuxent Parkway (at Harpers Farm Road)
Columbia, MD
(410) 772-4900
www.repstage.org
Ushers per performance: 4

The Rep Stage is a small professional theater housed on the Howard County
Community College campus outside of D.C. that has built a big reputation
for presenting quality productions of contemporary American plays and has
received numerous Helen Hayes awards. To usher, call the box office a week or
two in advance. Performances on Wednesday nights are Pay-What-You-Can.

Round House Theatre

4545 East-West Hwy. (between Pearl and Waverly Streets); Bethesda, MD
8641 Colesville Rd. (between Fenton Street and Georgia Avenue); Silver
Spring, MD
(240) 644-1099
volunteer@roundhousetheatre.org
www.round-house.org
Ushers per performance: 4 to 8 (depending on the venue)

The Round House is one of the leading professional theaters in the D.C. area
producing more then 200 performances per year on the main stage theater

in Bethesda and the black box theater in Silver Spring. Round House has built a national reputation for adapting literary works to the stage. It has a large and devoted following of ushers that sign up for a full season of ushering starting in the summer. Ushers sign up for dates as if it were a season subscription, so you are set to show up for a specific performance for each production (i.e., the second Saturday night of every production.) To sign up for an "ushering subscription," send an email expressing interest and the theater will let you know when sign-ups begin. You can also get on the on-call list to pick up a slot when there is a last-minute opening. There are also a number of other ways to see productions at the Round House for free (or seriously cheap). The first preview of every show on the main stage is Pay-What-You-Can. Tickets go on sale for this performance one hour before curtain. At the Silver Spring theater there are many free readings and performances throughout the year. Check out the Silver Spring page of the Web site for upcoming events.

Free Will

If you're a regular at the Shakespeare Theater Company, or you browse through The Folger for giggles and find yourself speaking in iambic pentameter at random times throughout the day, then you need to know about the **WillPower Festival at Montgomery College** every spring. This weeklong Shakespeare shebang is chock-full of performances, lectures, panel discussions, and workshops, and just about all events are free and open to everyone. For details check out the Web site www.montgomerycollege.edu/willpower.

Other free Shakespeare opportunities in the area include **the Shakespeare Theater's Free For All,** which takes place at the Harman Center (610 F St., NW between 6th and 7th Sts.) every September. Free tickets are given out on the day of the show at the box office (www.shakespearetheatre.org).

The **Olney Theatre** offers a free production at its complex (including free parking!) during the summer. Call for reservations and check the Web site for details (301-924-3400, www.olneytheatre.org).

Scena Theatre
(703) 684-7990
scena@scenatheatre.org
www.scenatheatre.org
Ushers per performance: 2 to 3

Scena produces a season of international plays that can range from Brecht and Beckett to contemporary European playwrights. There are performances in various theaters around D.C. If you are interested in ushering, call or send an email.

Shakespeare Theatre Company/Harman Center for the Arts
Lansburgh Theatre, 450 7th St., NW (between D and E Streets)
Sidney Harman Hall, 610 F St., NW (between 6th and 7th Sts.)
(202) 547-3230
www.shakespearetheatre.org
www.shakespearetheatre.org/harmancenter
Ushers per performance: 25 at the Harman Hall/11 at the Lansburgh Theatre

Shakespeare Theatre Company is one of the preeminent classical theater companies in the country—maybe even the world. It produces a full season of classical plays that range from re-imagined interpretations of Shakespeare (not surprisingly) to everything from Euripides to Noel Coward with the talent of some of the leading theater artists in the country. Volunteer ushers sign up to usher every show in the season, and in return they get quite a nice package of perks. In addition to seeing the productions at the STC, they also have the chance to see many of the music, dance, and theater performances that take place at the Harman Center. Ushers also get discounts at the gift shop and on classes, invitations to special events, and a chance to be a part of this top flight company. Keep an eye on the "Volunteer Ushering" page on the Harman Web site to find out when it is accepting applications. These spots are coveted, so get your application in immediately.

The STC also presents the Free-For-All, a free Shakespeare production every September at the Harman Hall. Every Wednesday at noon don't miss Happenings at the Harman, a free lunchtime series of music, dance, and theater performances.

Fringe Benefits

Every summer, every nook and cranny of The District is filled with performances that range from the outrageous and absurd to the daring and deeply moving when the **Capital Fringe Festival** takes over town for three weeks in July. The festival consists of more than 600 performances by more than 200 companies in 30 locations. Shows take place day and night, and Fringe needs help keeping the schedule moving along.

The life blood of Fringe is its volunteers, who do everything from working the box offices at venues and seating folks to building sets and any number of other helpful tasks. In return for your hard work, you get a voucher for free entry into any Fringe show and a cool T-shirt. If you commit to at least five shifts, you get one of the coveted buttons that get you loads of discounts and deals at nearby bars, restaurants, and other businesses not only during the festival, but throughout the year as well. To volunteer, fill out a form online, email, or stop by Fort Fringe during the festival. Capital Fringe Festival, 607 New York Avenue, NW (at 6th St.), (202) 737-7230, volunteer@capitalfringe.org, www.capitalfringe.org.

Signature Theatre

4200 Campbell Ave. (at 28th St.)
Arlington, VA
(571) 527-1860 (main phone)
(571) 527-1840 (usher hotline)
volunteer@signature-theatre.org
www.sig-online.org
Ushers per performance: 8 to 12

The Signature is the go-to place for musical theater in the D.C. area. The Tony-Award-winning theater is known for its often edgy, push-the-envelope productions of new musicals and reinterpretations of established shows, particularly Sondheim musicals. The theater recently swept the Helen Hayes Awards for its small-scale/big-hearted version of *Les Misérables*. The theater is very popular, so volunteer ushering slots can be hard to come by. To join the corps of volunteers who commit to ushering for every show of the season, fill out an application on the Web site. If there is an opening, you can pick a specific night of the week to usher for every show, and you will be scheduled as each show rolls around. There are also a number of other freebies like panel talks, readings, and various events throughout the year. See the theater's listing in Always Free for more details.

Spooky Action Theater

Georgia Ave. and East West Hwy.
Takoma Park, MD
(301) 920-1414
www.spookyaction.org
Ushers per performance: 2 to 3

This small professional company based out of Montgomery College produces literate works with energy and exuberant physicality. To usher, call at the beginning of the week to set it up. The first three or four previews are Pay-What-You-Can, and the theater also presents a number of staged readings and workshops of new plays throughout the year. Check the Web site or call for details.

The Studio Theatre

1501 14th St., NW (between P and Church Streets)
(202) 232-7267
usher@studiotheatre.org
www.studiotheatre.org
Ushers per performance: 10

The Studio Theatre is one of the big shots of the D.C. theater scene. The company has a national reputation for presenting energetic works of contemporary plays, musicals, and unexpected revivals including everything from the plays of Tom Stoppard and Neil Labute to *Jerry Springer: The Opera*. Ushers work a variety of positions at the performances including taking tickets, working the bar, and checking coats. Email the theater at least a week in advance to set up a date. Ushers also get half price on all concessions, except alcohol. The Pay-What-You-Can evening is the first Saturday performance of every show. The Second Stage at the theater also produces a series of free staged readings at various times throughout the year.

Synetic Theatre

1611 N Kent St. (between Wilson Boulevard and 19ᵗʰ St. N)
Arlington, VA
(703) 824-8061
synetic@synetictheater.org
Ushers per performance: 4

Synetic produces classical theater, but in a distinctly unclassical way. The shows, infused with music, movement, dance, and mime, are unlike any other you've likely seen (there are not many theaters that can successfully produce a silent *Hamlet,* but Synetic did). Each season the theater continues to produce performances that are decidedly different. It uses volunteer ushers at performances held at the Roslyn Spectrum (not the spring productions at the Kennedy Center). Try to contact the theater about usher openings about six weeks ahead of time, but you can also try your luck up to a week before the date you want to attend. It also has a Pay-What-You-Can performance the last preview before opening, usually on a Thursday night.

Theater J

Washington D.C. Jewish Community Center
1529 16th St. NW (between Q and Church Streets)
(202) 777-3210
theaterj@theaterj.org
www.washingtondcjcc.org/center-for-arts/theater-j
Ushers per performance: 4

Theater J produces plays and events that start from a Jewish or Middle Eastern theme but then often shoot off in unexpected directions. The plays are more edgy and provocative than you might expect at the JCC. To usher, email or call two weeks to a month before to make a reservation. The theater also brings in nationally known performers such as Sandra Bernhard and Theodore Bikel. After shows on Thursday nights and Sunday afternoons, free panel discussions are held that may be vaguely related to the show but are also interesting standalone events. Pay-What-You-Can performances are the first two previews of every show, except the big-name performers.

Washington Shakespeare Company

Clark Street Playhouse
601 South Clark St. (between 6th and 10th Sts. S)
Arlington, VA
(703) 418-4808
www.washingtonshakespeare.org
Ushers per performance: 2 to 3

If you were not able to get an ushering reservation at the Shakespeare Theater, you should have no problem meeting your daily requirement of Shakespeare and other classics at the Washington Shakespeare Company. This theater is pretty casual about ushering. Call and if you catch someone on the phone, you're in for any show you want. If you don't reach a human being, keep calling; the theater is shorthanded and can use your help.

Washington Stage Guild

The Mead Theatre Lab at Flashpoint
916 G St., NW (between 9th and 10th Sts.)
info@stageguild.org
(240) 582-0050
www.stageguild.org
Ushers per performance: 4

The Stage Guild is the home of intelligent and literate theater in D.C. All seasons include plays by the likes of Jean Cocteau, Ferenc Molnar, Oscar Wilde, and especially George Bernard Shaw, as well as a mix of more contemporary literate playwrights. Call or email to get on the ushering list. A notice that the theater is accepting reservations goes out for every show. All previews are Pay-What-You-Can. There are also free readings about once a month. The Washington Stage Guild is in the process of building its own theater that it hopes to be moving into soon, so check to confirm address and other details.

Woolly Mammoth Theater Company

641 D St., NW (between 6th and 7th Sts.)
(202) 289-2443
tommesha@woollymammoth.net
www.woollymammoth.net
Ushers per performance: 6 to 8

"Provocative," "Inventive," "Smart," "Wacked-out," "Daring," "Exhilarating," "One-of-a-kind" are just some of the superlatives used to describe the unexpected performances seen year after year at the Woolly Mammoth. Many of the plays developed and premiered here go on to be performed in theaters all around the world. To usher, send an email asking to join the ushering list. The theater tries to sign folks up for a full year of ushering at the beginning of every season, generally in August. You can also try any time to see if there is an opening for specific shows. In addition, the theater makes 10 Stampede tickets available the night of the show for $15, and the first two performances of every show are Pay-What-You-Can performances.

ALWAYS FREE

Charter Theatre
Arts Club of Washington
2017 I St., NW (between 20th and 21st Sts.)
(202) 333-7009
www.chartertheatre.org

Charter's mission is to develop new plays by D.C.-based playwrights. As part of the development process, it runs a series of play readings usually on Tuesday evenings once a month. Check the Web site for a schedule of upcoming readings.

Happenings at the Harman
Shakespeare Theatre Company/Harman Center for the Arts
Sidney Harman Hall, 610 F St., NW (between 6th and 7th Sts.)
(202) 547-3230
www.shakespearetheatre.org

The Harman Center presents a free series of music, dance, and theater performances every Wednesday at noon. No need for reservations, just show up and enjoy.

Journeymen Theater

Church Street Theater
1742 Church St., NW (between 17th and 18th and Q and P Streets)
(202) 669-7229
www.journeymentheater.org

Join Journeymen for a series of free readings of new plays on the morning of the second Saturday of every month. Check the Web site for location and details.

Metro Stage

1201 North Royal St. (between Bashford Lane and Third Street)
Alexandria, VA
(703) 548-9044
www.metrostage.org

Metro Stage mostly produces musicals, as well as some plays. Sporadically throughout the year, it presents free readings of new musicals and plays. The best way to find out about its offerings is to sign up for the email list on its Web site.

National Conservatory of Dramatic Arts

1556 Wisconsin Avenue, NW (between Volta Place and Q Street)
(202) 333-2202
NFicca@TheConservatory.org

The National Conservatory is a conservatory training program. The program attracts aspiring actors from around the country and gives them plenty of opportunities to hone their skills in the many student productions presented throughout the year. All of the student productions are free. The Conservatory also teams up with some theater companies around the D.C. area, and they generally ask for a suggested donation of $15 for those productions. The tickets to the student productions are free, but it's a good idea to call or email to reserve your seats. Check out the Web site for the schedule of performances.

National Theatre

1321 Pennsylvania Ave., NW (between 13th and 14th Sts.)
(202) 783-3372
www.nationaltheatre.org

Most nights this historic theater plays host to pricy Broadway road shows and other high-profile performances, and no, sorry, we can't quite get you into those for free, but on Monday nights and Saturday mornings it turns into a freebie free-for-all. Every Monday night at 6 and 7:30 you will find performances that could be anything from magic to cabaret shows, from ethnic dance recitals to original plays. And on Saturday mornings at 9:30 & 11 you will find a similar mix of productions geared to a younger audience of children three and up. The performances take place in the theater's Helen Hayes Gallery. During the summer, you can escape the heat with its film series every Monday night at 6:30. All shows are free, but tickets are required. Tickets are handed out a half-hour before showtime on a first-come, first-served basis.

Shakespeare Theatre Company/Harman Center for the Arts
Sidney Harman Hall
610 F St. NW (between 6th and 7th Sts.)
(202) 547-3230
www.shakespearetheatre.org

The STC also presents the Free-For-All, a free Shakespeare production every September at the Harman Hall. These productions include all the bells and whistles of the STC's mainstage productions including stellar casts, directors, and production elements. Tickets are handed out at the box office two hours before the performance.

Signature Theatre
4200 Campbell Ave. (at 28th St.)
Arlington, VA
(571) 527-1860
www.sig-online.org

You can get to know the talent behind the productions at the Signature and peek behind the scenes at two free casual discussions held each month with the performers, writers, or directors of the productions currently running at the theater. Sometimes the theater takes the opportunity to present readings of new material it is developing. On the first Monday of each month *From Page to Stage* takes place at the **Shirlington Library** (4200 Campbell Avenue) from 7 to 8 p.m. On the first Thursday of each month *Brown Bag Lunch* (lunch not included, sorry!) takes place at the theater from 1 to 2 p.m. Every August it hosts an open house with performances, workshops, and lectures and good times for all.

The Theatre Lab School of the Dramatic Arts

733 8th St., NW (between G and H Streets)
(202) 824-0449
www.theatrelab.org

Once or twice a year the school partners with a professional company in D.C. (Woolly Mammoth, Theater J. or others) to produce a series of four free readings. The readings team a group of advanced students with a professional director and performer from the company. The series usually takes place in the spring but sometimes also in the fall. Check its Web site for the schedule.

Young Playwrights' Theater

2437 15th St., NW (between Euclid and Chapin Streets)
(202) 387-9173
www.youngplaywrightstheater.org

Young Playwrights' Theater pairs professional actors, writers, and directors with student playwrights from the D.C. school system to create some surprisingly compelling works. Throughout the school year it presents many readings, workshops, and performances and most are completely free. **The New Writers Now!** series of readings happens about once a month on a Monday night and usually includes three to five short plays, a catered reception, and a talk-back with the artists. The performances take place at various theaters around town, so check out its Web site for details and a schedule of performances throughout the year.

DRAMA DEALS: DISCOUNT TICKETS

Every now and then, there may come a time when you want to see a show that does not have a free option. Well, fear not, there are plenty of ways to slip into a show for a pittance at many of the leading D.C. theaters.

Ticket Place Booth

407 7th St., NW (between D & E Streets)
www.ticketplace.org
Open Tuesday to Friday from 11 a.m. to 6 p.m., Saturday 10 a.m. to 5 p.m.

The Catch Half-priced tickets plus a 12 percent service charge on the full price of the ticket.

You can purchase half-priced tickets to many shows at venues such as Arena Stage, Kennedy Center, Folger Theater, Ford's Theatre, National Geographic, and others. In addition to plays and musicals, the offerings often include music, dance, opera, and film. You can pick up day-of-the-show tickets at the booth or online and advanced tickets at the booth.

Goldstar.com

The Catch Half-priced tickets plus a service charge ($3 to $7 per ticket)

Sign up for free membership to this Web site, and you will have access to half-priced tickets to a large selection of performances and events throughout the D.C. area. You will find tickets not only to many of D.C.'s theaters but also to baseball games, concerts, seminars, and other surprising events. You do need to be a member to buy the tickets, but membership is free. The site charges a sliding-scale service charge on top of the half price, generally between $3 and $7 per ticket. The site includes useful tips like where to find free parking and reviews from members who have seen the show.

MUSIC:
OF FREE I SING

"Will the people in the cheaper seats clap your hands? And the rest of you, if you'll just rattle your jewelry."
—JOHN LENNON

D.C. is overflowing with free music from street corner or metro platform to museums, embassies, clubs, bars, churches, parks, and concert halls. You don't have to look very far to find the strains of any style of music: Classical, Rock, Jazz, Country, Folk, Experimental, World, Ethnic. If you can hum it, you can find it somewhere in D.C. for free. The city's museums are a rich source of free concerts for classical, regional, and international music lovers. The summer months are particularly inviting, with free performances and concert series around the district. Bars and clubs also offer free shows but may charge hefty drink minimums.

ROCK/POP/FOLK/ALTERNATIVE

Fire Flies
1501 Mount Vernon Ave. (at East Nelson Avenue)
Alexandria, VA
(703) 548-7200
www.firefliesdelray.com

On almost any night, the music flows at this Del Ray restaurant and wine bar. The schedule includes a great mix of local musicians playing folk, blues, and bluegrass.

The Harp & Fiddle
4844 Cordell Ave. (between Woodmont and Norfolk Avenues)
Bethesda, MD
(301) 951-0115
www.flanagansharpandfiddle.com

The Catch A small cover charge on the weekends.

This Irish pub showcases rock, funk, electric blues, and traditional Irish music. The volume is usually pumped up pretty high here, so if you're looking for some quiet background music, this is not the place for you. The shows during the week are free, but they do charge a small cover for their most popular performers on the weekends, usually around $5.

Irish Times

14 F St. NW (between North Capitol Street and North Mccollough Court)
(202) 534-5344
www.petepapageorge.com

It's a dive bar, and it embraces the fact. The Irish Times brings in a crowd of college students and kickball enthusiasts to sing along with D.C. musical institution Pete Papageorge. Papageorge has been performing sing-along favorites such as "Sweet Caroline," "Brown Eyed Girl," and the MTA song almost every Friday and Saturday night since 1985.

McGinty's Public House

911 Ellsworth Dr. (between Fenton Street and Georgia Avenue)
Silver Spring, MD
(301) 587-1270
www.mcgintyspublichouse.com

The Catch A small cover charge on Friday and Saturday nights.

On the weekends, McGinty's charges you a few bucks to dance to their loud cover bands upstairs, but during the week it's a different story. Tuesday nights serve up an authentic Irish session. Bring your own instrument to join in or just enjoy the traditional tunes. On Thursdays local musicians play original and popular acoustic tunes. Sunday nights feature swing dance lessons from 6 to 8 p.m., which are offered at a nominal charge, but you are free to dance for free from 8 to 10 p.m. The proprietors are opening a new location in Arlington (3650 South Glebe Rd., 703-414-3555) that will have a similar schedule.

Mr. Henry's Capitol Hill

601 Pennsylvania Ave. SE (at 6th Street)
(202) 546-8412
www.mrhenrysrestaurant.com

Mr. Henry's has a long history of giving talented musicians a start—singer Roberta Flack began a long run as the resident performer in the 1960s. Nowadays, the in-house musical wonder is Milan Sweet, whom you can see performing his soulful tunes on Thursday nights.

Ramparts Tavern and Grill

1700 Fern St.
Alexandria, VA
(703) 998-6616
www.rampsrest.com

As you can tell by the name, music is not the highest priority here, but Ramparts does showcase local rock bands Tuesdays to Saturday nights and never charges a cover or minimum.

Sixth & I Historic Synagogue

600 I St., NW (at I Street)
(202) 408-3100
nprixel@sixthandi.org
www.sixthandi.org

The Catch Volunteer for free entry to performances.

Become an "Ambassador" (aka volunteer usher) to see shows at the Sixth & I Historic Synagogue for free. Not all shows are Jewish-centric, however; the synagogue books a diverse blend of performers, including indie-rock bands, Comedy Central comedians, and old-school mix. Recent shows included Sandra Bernhard, Antony and the Johnstons, Rob Riggle, and Kris Kristofferson.

To become an Ambassador you sit through a short orientation at the venue. Then, the synagogue sends e-mails monthly for upcoming events. Submit your requests and the organizers will let you know within the week if they need you. In addition to seeing shows for free, Ambassadors rack up some other perks, such as free tee shirts and other Sixth & I gear, occasional comps to shows, and Ambassador-appreciation parties throughout the year.

Sova

1359 H St., NE (between 13th and 14th Streets)
(202) 397-3080
www.sovadc.com

This laid-back Capitol Hill coffeehouse and wine bar presents a handful of shows every month that are almost all free. The shows take place in its second floor performance space at which music aficionados enjoy local folk, jazz, and bluegrass artists.

Hit the Streets

What's wrong, you can't swing the $250 tickets to that Springsteen show (and that's far from the most expensive tickets!)? Well, don't let that stop you from catching all the big shows at venues such as the Warner Theater, Verizon Center, Nissan Pavilion, and the 9:30 Club. Join their **Street Teams** and you're in for nothing! Street Team members hang up posters for concerts, dispense flyers at clubs, post ads on their Facebook pages, etc. to get the word out about upcoming shows. Each venue has its own system for working with Street Teams, but just about every club and concert hall has one. The best candidates are hooked into the club and music scene but can also get the job done. Once you establish yourself with a club, you might even see some unexpected tickets and swag head your way. Here is a list of venues and how to get in touch to join their Street Team. If you're interested in a club that is not on this list, get in touch with them; they probably have one.

The Warner Theater, Nissan Pavilion, Verizon Center, and Patriot Center are all run by Live Nation: E-mail them through their Facebook page: Live Nation—D.C.

9:30 Club: Send them an e-mail to list_serve@930.com.

The State Theater: Send them an e-mail at streetteam@thestate theatre.com.

University of Maryland

Stamp Student Union
Campus Drive and Union Lane
College Park, MD
(301) 405-0569
www.see.umd.edu
freestuff.umd.edu

College is not just for students anymore. Every semester the UMD–College Park showcases an unpredictable mix of free performances from indie and folk rock to hip-hop and international and classical. The Student Entertainment Events bring in some recognizable names, and many other student and faculty performances always occur.

JAZZ/BLUES/HIP-HOP/WORLD

Archie Edward Blues Barbershop
4701 Queensbury Rd. (at Lafayette Avenue); Prince George's, MD
Bangkok Blues, 926 West Broad St. (between Washington and West Streets);
Falls Church, VA
(201) 396-3504
www.acousticblues.com

Once in a while you come across something so wonderful, pure, and unadulterated, you're afraid to tell others about it for fear of its becoming too popular. This is one of those things.

Archie Edwards was a master bluesman and barber who held informal blues jams every Saturday afternoon in his barbershop. For more than fifty years, musicians of all levels, including blues legends such as Mississippi John Hurt and Skip James, would stop by to play the Piedmont blues with Edwards. Edwards passed away in 1998, but the Archie Edwards Blues Heritage Foundation continues the Saturday tradition. Until 2008 they gathered at his old barbershop, but today they have recreated the barbershop, complete with Archie's old barber chairs and mirrors, at a Riverdale bookstore. The music begins at 2:30 p.m. every Saturday and continues until 6 p.m. It's a casual affair—no one person leads the show, but everyone, from the professionals to the novices, jams together. Visitors are welcome to bring their own instruments to take part in the fun. The jam moves to Bangkok Blues in Falls Church on Sunday evenings.

Bossa
2463 18th Street, NW (between North Adams Mill and North Belmont Roads)
(202) 667-0088
www.bossaproject.com

The Catch Small cover charge after 10 p.m.

Bossa somehow manages to be a laid-back, sultry lounge while also still being a pulsing, pick-uppy, dance club. The live salsa and Latin jazz starts at 10 every night, so get there early to avoid the cover charge ($3 to $5) after 10 p.m.

Café Citron
1345 Connecticut Ave., NW (off Dupont Circle)
(202) 530-8844
www.cafecitrondc.com

The crowds throng to this Latin music for salsa dancing. With no cover charge, it understandably gets crowded fast. After 10 p.m. it's not unusual to see a line down the block, especially on the weekends, so be sure to dress to impress the picky doorman. Don't miss the live flamenco performances on Monday nights at 9 p.m.; Tuesdays features a live salsa band starting at 7 p.m.; and there are free salsa dance lessons on Saturdays at 8:30 p.m.

Chief Ike's Mambo Room
1725 Columbia Rd., NW
(202) 332-2211
www.chiefikesmamboroom.com

This local favorite showcases reggae bands, hip-hop performers and other musicians on Tuesday and Wednesday nights. DJs spin dance tunes the rest of the week. No cover Sunday to Wednesday or before 10 p.m. on other nights.

Eighteenth Street Lounge
1212 18th St., NW
(202) 466-3922
www.eighteenthstreetlounge.com

The Catch Cover charge on some nights, unless they like the look of you.

This converted Dupont Circle townhouse mansion is a swanky and at times exclusive club. The Eighteenth Street Lounge attracts an international crowd, and the music is just as worldly: reggae, Brazilian, hip-hop, funk, and salsa. No cover charge on Tuesday, Thursday, or Sunday nights; as much as $20 the rest of the week, although if you're charming and good-looking, you may get in for nothing.

La Tasca Spanish Restaurant
607 King St. (between South Washington and North Asaph Streets)
Alexandria, VA
(703) 299-9810
www.latascausa.com

On Friday nights the spirit of flamenco dance comes alive at 7:30 p.m. and 8:30 p.m. At 10 p.m. Duende Cameron, Alexandria's answer to the Gipsy Kings, takes the stage for a high energy evening of live flamenco music. Shimmy to the Latin rock sounds of local band Deep Dreams on Saturdays.

Meridian Hill Park Drumming Circle
16th and Euclid Streets, NW
www.malcolmxdrummersanddancers.blogspot.com

Every Sunday people converge on Meridian Hill Park to surrender to the beat. The drumming circle in the park (also known as Malcolm X Park) has been a tradition for more than forty years and shows no sign of slowing down. The circle, consisting of the Malcolm X Drummers and Dancers, runs from 3 to 9 p.m. every Sunday, weather permitting. It's a subdued affair in the afternoon, but as the crowd of drummers and dancers swells, the rhythm builds to a frenzy. Feel free to join in.

Smithsonian American Art Museum
8th and F Streets, NW
(202) 633-1000
www.americanart.si.edu

Take a load off after work in the glorious Kogod Courtyard of the museum. Take 5 is a series of jazz concerts on the third Thursday of the month from 5 to 8 p.m.

Tryst Coffeehouse
2459 18th St., NW (between Columbia and Kalorama Road)
(202) 232-5500
www.trystdc.com

Local artists' paintings adorn the walls, the cappuccino machine growls, as customers recline on mismatched sofas and comfy chairs to enjoy the free Wi-Fi at this Adams Morgan hangout. Relax on Monday, Tuesday, or Wednesday nights, and enjoy the jazz music as you sip a pricey café au lait (at least they throw in some free animal crackers).

Zoo Bar
3000 Connecticut Ave., NW (at North Hawthorne Street)
(202) 232-4225
www.zoobardc.com

A perfect marriage of authentic blues and a true dive bar. Each Thursday is an open mic blues jam, and Friday and Saturday nights showcase bands, all without a cover charge.

CLASSICAL/STANDARDS/CABARET

American University
4400 Massachusetts Ave. (at Nebraska Avenue)
(202) 885-3634
www.american.edu/cas/performing-arts

On select Thursday afternoons during the school year, enjoy classical concerts at the The Atrium Series. The series brings noted local and visiting musicians to the American University campus for free concerts that are open to all. The shows take place at noon at the Battelle-Tompkins Atrium, located across from the sports center and amphitheater.

Anderson House
2118 Massachusetts Ave., NW (between 21st and 22nd Streets)
(202) 785-2040
www.societyofthecincinnati.org

In the spring and fall, the Society of the Cincinnati invites you into the elegant ballroom at the Anderson House for concerts by soloists and small ensembles on Saturday afternoons.

Church of the Epiphany
1317 G St., NW (between 13th and 14th Streets)
(202) 347-2635
www.epiphanydc.org

The Church of the Epiphany hosts classical concerts featuring D.C.-based musicians and ensembles every Tuesday at noon. Regular contributors include the Washington Bach Consort, Levine School of Music and World Sounds Downtown. The concerts are free, but they do ask for donations for the musicians.

Duke Ellington School of the Arts
3500 R St., NW (at 35th Street)
(202) 282-0123
www.ellingtonschool.org

Washington's version of *Fame,* this public high school trains students for careers in music, theater, dance, and the visual arts. Most performances aren't free except for student recitals and other concerts.

Freer and Sackler Galleries
1150 Jefferson Dr., SW (at 12th Street)
(202) 633-1000
www.asia.si.edu

The Catch You will need to pay a small service fee in order to make advanced reservations.

Asian musicians and groups often showcase their talents in concert at the Freer and Sackler Galleries. Tickets are free and dispensed one hour before showtime. Ticketmaster charges a service fee to reserve tickets in advance. Generally, if you get there as they start handing out tickets, you won't have a problem getting in.

The Friday Morning Music Club
Various locations
(202) 333-2075
www.fmmc.org

Contrary to what the name implies, The Friday Morning Music Club doesn't limit its concerts to Friday mornings. Solo artists, chamber groups, and orchestras perform throughout the week at various locations in D.C., Maryland, and Virginia. Concerts take place throughout the year, primarily on Tuesdays, Thursdays, and Fridays with more choices from October until May.

Georgetown University
McNeir Hall
37th and O Street, NW (behind Dahlgren Chapel)
(202) 687-3838
http://performingarts.georgetown.edu/music/FridayMusicConcertSeries
Internationally acclaimed visiting artists perform classical, opera, and dance

every Friday at 1:15 p.m. during the school year. No tickets or reservations required.

Happenings at the Harman
Sidney Harman Hall
610 F St., NW (at 6th Street)
(202) 547-1122
www.shakespearetheatre.org/harmancenter

Classical music, modern dance, theater, and other performers working the stages of the Harman Center at night are featured in more informal afternoon performances every Wednesday at noon. No tickets or reservations required.

IBIS Chamber Music Society
Various locations
(703) 527-3960
www.ibischambermusic.org

The IBIS Chamber Music Society is composed of members of the Kennedy Center Orchestra, the National Symphony, and the Boston Pops, performing on harp, flute, and string quartet. The concerts are friendly and informal, with programming ranging from Beethoven to Brubeck. Stay for the wine and cheese meet-and-greet post-concert reception.

Levine School of Music
2801 Upton St., NW (between Connecticut Avenue and Linnean Avenue)
1901 Mississippi Ave., SE (between 18th and 19th Streets)
5301 Tuckerman Lane, North Bethesda (off Rockville Pike)
1125 North Patrick Henry Dr., Arlington (between 11th Street North and Washington Boulevard)
(202) 686-8000
www.levineschool.org

The Catch Some concerts are not free.

The Levine School of Music offers music classes and lessons and has spread its good works over many different communities throughout the D.C. region. The school also showcases performances and community events in four different locations throughout the year. While the classes and lessons are not free, many of the performances are. Enjoy faculty concerts, student recitals, and master classes with internationally renowned artists such as Yo-Yo Ma. One regularly scheduled free performance is Lunch with Levine the second Tuesday of the month at the Church of the Epiphany.

The Library of Congress
101 Independence Ave., SE (between 1st Street and South Capitol Street)
(202) 707-5000 (general information)
(202) 707-5502 (concert information)
www.loc.gov

The Catch Tickets are required for many performances. They are free, but Ticketmaster charges a service fee if you order them in advance.

The Library of Congress has a full schedule of performances, lectures, and films. Every Friday night at 8 p.m. celebrated soloists and small ensembles perform in the Coolidge Auditorium, and many other classical concerts happen throughout the week. Check out the Home Grown concerts at the American Folk Life Center. The center presents American regional and folk performers on weekday afternoons once or twice a month. Tickets, which are free, are required for many of these performances, including the Friday night concerts. To avoid Ticketmaster service fees, opt for standby tickets, which are distributed beginning at 6:30 p.m. on the night of a show.

Millennium Stage
Kennedy Center for the Performing Arts
25th St., NW near F Street
(202) 467-4600
www.kennedy-center.org

The granddaddy of free performances in D.C., The Millennium Stage offers a wide range of performances every day of the year beginning at 6 p.m. As one would expect, you're likely to see classical music, jazz, musical theater, dance, and opera, but it doesn't stop there. It's not unusual to see Mexican rock bands, children's theater, experimental or international folk music. Most performances take place in the grand foyer of the Kennedy Center but often move to other venues within the complex depending on the needs of the performance.

The Music Center at Strathmore

5301 Tuckerman Lane (off Rockville Pike)
North Bethesda, MD
(301) 581-5200
www.strathmore.org

The Catch *Volunteers must commit to usher three times a month.*

The Music Center at Strathmore is home to the Baltimore Symphony Orchestra, National Philharmonic, Washington Performing Art Society as well as other arts organizations. You can attend any performance by these and other visiting artists and groups by becoming a volunteer usher. Volunteers must be willing to usher at least three times a month and take part in an orientation. On the night of the show, ushers show up ninety minutes before showtime to help seat the concertgoers and will be on duty for either the first or second half of the performance.

National Gallery of Art

4th and Constitution Avenues, NW (between 3rd and 9th Streets)
(202) 737-4215
www.nga.gov

The Sunday evening concerts at the National Gallery of Art's west garden courtyard are one of D.C.'s greatest pleasures. Internationally celebrated musicians and ensembles fill the courtyard with music for all to enjoy. Many other classical concerts are scheduled every month at the museum, and during the summer you can enjoy jazz concerts in the sculpture garden. No tickets required; seating is on a first-come, first-served basis, so arrive early.

Smithsonian American Art Museum

8th and F Streets NW
(202) 633-1000
www.americanart.si.edu

The museum presents concerts on the second Sunday of every month utilizing SAAM's refurbished Steinway concert grand piano.

University of Maryland School of Music

2110 Clarice Smith Performing Arts Center
College Park, MD
(301) 405-5549 (administrative office)
(301) 405-2787 (box office)
www.music.umd.edu
www.freestuff.umd.edu

The University of Maryland School of Music presents a variety of free performances every school year, including concerts by the large student ensembles (Wind Orchestra, UM Symphony Orchestra, the Repertoire Orchestra, and the Men's and Women's Chorus), smaller groups, and student and faculty recitals. Many of the performances take place in Dekelboum Concert Hall or the more intimate Gildenhorn Recital Hall. No tickets are required for the free shows, just show up fifteen to thirty minutes prior to the performance.

MILITARY BANDS

The four branches of the military each have their own bands based in D.C. These groups do much more than play "Stars and Stripes Forever." Each of the bands also splits into smaller performing units specializing in jazz, blues, vocal harmony, and rock. One is just as likely to hear these bands play the music of Frank Zappa or Count Basie as one is to hear "Anchors Aweigh."

U.S. Air Force Band

Various locations
(202) 767-5658
www.usafband.af.mil

Known as America's International Musical Ambassadors, the Air Force Band includes six separate performing units: The Singing Sergeants, Air Force Strings, the jazz ensemble Airmen of Note, the Ceremonial Brass, Max Impact, and the full concert band. In the summer, the band performs at the Air Force Memorial. During the rest of the year, it performs at the Jazz Heritage Series, at chamber performances throughout the region, and with popular guest artists such as Patti LaBelle and Clint Black.

U.S. Army Band

Various locations
(703) 696-3399
www.usarmyband.com

"Pershing's Own" consists of eight performing units, including the troupe Army Blues, the choral ensemble Down Range, and brass and string ensembles. The full band and the separate units perform at many venues in the area throughout the year. During the summer don't miss Twilight Tattoo, a military pageant tracing the history of the army, at Fort McNair every Wednesday night, and the Sunsets with a Soundtrack concerts on the steps of the Capitol on Friday nights.

U.S. Marine Band

Various locations
(202) 433-4011(general concert info)
(202) 433-6060 (evening parade info)
www.marineband.usmc.mil
www.mbw.usmc.mil (for reservations to the Evening Parade)

Established in 1798, "The President's Own" Marine Band is the nation's oldest professional musical organization. Its musicians also make up the Marine Chamber Orchestra and Marine Chamber Ensembles. They perform regularly at White House state dinners and official events, as well as other venues in the D.C. region. The band features the music of John Philip Sousa, as well as a mix of other classical and contemporary tunes. During the summer months, the band performs around the city, including on the Capitol steps on Thursday evenings and at the Washington Memorial on Friday nights at sunset. Don't miss the Evening Parade at the Marine Barracks (8th and I Streets, SE) starting at 8:45 p.m. on Fridays during the summer. It's a rousing display of precision marching and formations set to music. The parade requires reservations. On Tuesday evenings in the summer you can observe the more somber Sunset Parade at the Iwo Jima Memorial in Arlington National Cemetery.

U.S. Navy Band

Various locations
(202) 433-2525
www.navyband.navy.mil

The Navy Band consists of smaller performing units such as the Sea Chanters chorus, the jazz ensemble The Commodores, the country-bluegrass group

Country Current, and The Cruisers, who perform contemporary music. The full band and its smaller offshoots perform year-round in the D.C. area. In the summer you can catch them every Monday night at the Capitol building and Tuesday evenings at the Navy Memorial.

SUMMER CONCERTS

Brookside Gardens
1800 Glenallan Ave. (just off Randolph Road)
Wheaton, MD
(301) 962-1400
www.brooksidegardens.org

The Twilight Concert Series takes place each Tuesday evening in June at 6:30 p.m. at Brookside's Guide Garden. The concerts vary from week to week with everything on tap from rockabilly to roots rock to jazz standards.

Carter Barron Amphitheatre
16th Street and Colorado Avenue, NW
(202) 426-0486
www.nps.gov/rocr/planyourvisit/cbarron.htm

The Catch Only half the shows are free.

Every summer for the past fifty years, Washingtonians and visitors have gathered at the Carter Barron Amphitheatre to enjoy performances under the stars. About half of the shows are free, and the others will run you about $25 apiece. The free shows include many genres of music, but if you're lucky you may get to see the National Symphony Orchestra, local and national rock bands, and the D.C. Blues Society. Some free shows do require tickets, which are distributed on the day of the show at the box office from noon to 8 p.m.

Fairfax County Summer Entertainment Series

Various locations throughout Fairfax County
www.fairfaxcounty.gov/parks/performances

Fairfax County schedules a full set of performances, concerts, and movies that take place in various locations throughout the county. Concerts include big band, jazz, bluegrass, folk, and classical music.

Fort Reno Park Summer Music Series

3800 Donaldson Place, NW
(703) 318-2197
www.fortreno.com

For more than thirty years Tenleytown has been turning the volume way up at these twice-weekly concerts featuring indie-rock and hardcore bands. The concerts are strictly alcohol free and draw a big crowd of underage rockers. Some complain that the concerts have become a bit tame in recent years, but the residents of Donaldson Place would have to disagree. June through August.

Friday Night Live!

777 Lynn St.
Herndon, VA
(703) 481-6133

Herndon rocks on Friday nights with big crowds enjoying local cover and tribute bands on the town green. May through August.

Jazz in the Garden

National Gallery of Art
7th Street and Constitution Avenue, NW
(202) 289-3360
www.nga.gov/programs/jazz

Spread out a blanket, unpack the picnic goodies, and relax to the groove of some of D.C.'s and the country's finest jazz musicians every Friday evening at the National Gallery's sculpture garden. The concerts run from late May to the beginning of October at 5 p.m.

Live! on Woodrow Wilson Plaza

Ronald Reagan Building
1300 Pennsylvania Ave., NW
www.itcdc.com

Enjoy all genres of music at these popular lunchtime concerts every weekday from June through September. From salsa to swing, hip-hop to blues, the series features popular local and world-renowned performers in a relaxing, open-air atmosphere. And don't miss the finale with the city's own Godfather of Go-Go, Chuck Brown.

The Music Center at Strathmore

5301 Tuckerman Lane (off Rockville Pike)
North Bethesda, MD
(301) 581-5200
www.strathmore.org

On Wednesday evenings the music moves outdoors at the Music Center of Strathmore for free concerts at the Gudelsky Concert Pavilion. The concerts range from big band to classical and standards. Mid-June to Mid-August.

Strike Up the Band!

Continuing a tradition that dates back to 1863, every summer the military bands of the Army, Navy, Marines and Air Force perform stirring concerts in the shadows of some of the capital's most iconic locations. The bands perform on the west lawn of the Capitol building, at the Washington Monument, and at the Lincoln and Air Force memorials on alternating days. Each band also maintains a full schedule of concerts throughout the year; check out the Military Bands section on pages 37–39 for more information. The outdoor concerts run from June through August.

Silver Spring Swings & Downtown Concert Series

Silver Plaza (Ellsworth Drive between Georgia Avenue and Fenton Street)
Silver Spring, MD
(301) 565-7300 (Thursday concerts)
(301) 587-0867 (Friday and Saturday concerts)
www.silverspringdowntown.com
www.downtownsilverspring.com

Bring the family to downtown Silver Spring, Maryland, every Thursday, Friday, and Saturday night to enjoy salsa, zydeco, rock, funk, reggae, and more. And it is not just the music that's free; kids enjoy the free face painting and prizes while their parents enjoy gift certificate raffles. Mid-June to mid-August.

Sounds in the Square

Connecticut Avenue and K St., NW
(202) 463-3400
www.gtbid.com
www.myspace.com/soundsinthesquare

Popular local country, rock, or pop bands perform in Farragut Square Park every Thursday evening in June and July.

Sunset Serenades at the National Zoo

3100 Connecticut Ave., NW (near Cathedral Avenue)
(202) 633-4800
www.nationalzoo.si.edu

Family-friendly jazz, folk, blues, and rock 'n' roll concerts every Thursday evening in July and August at the Lion/Tiger Hill.

TGIF Summer Concert Series

Wheaton Triangle (Georgia Avenue and Veirs Mill Road)
(240) 777-8106
www.wheatonmd.org

The TGIF Summer Concert Series features a different genre of music every performance, from salsa to big band to zydeco or roots rock. The concerts take place on the second and fourth Friday of the month, June through August.

Wolf Trap

1551 Trap Rd. (off SR 267, Dulles Toll Road)
Vienna, VA
(703) 255-1893
www.nps.gov/wotr (volunteer info under Support Your Park)
www.wolftrap.org (performance information)

The Catch Must commit to volunteer usher one night a week during the concert season.

An evening at Wolf Trap is one of the most magical experiences you can have in the area, with the stars glimmering from above and on stage. Each summer, Wolf Trap puts together an eclectic schedule of performers and events such as Elvis Costello, Bill Cosby, Tony Bennett, *A Prairie Home Companion, Riverdance,* and Merce Cunningham Dance Company. Get into the shows for free by applying to be a volunteer usher. Ushers must commit to helping out one night a week during the season. Generally ushers check in about an hour before showtime, help seat the paying customers, and enjoy the show. Apply through a link on the National Park Service Web site above.

FILM:
CHEAP SHOTS

"I have the terrible feeling that, because I am wearing a white beard and am sitting in the back of the theatre, you expect me to tell you the truth about something. These are the cheap seats, not Mount Sinai."
—ORSON WELLES

Now that the average movie ticket costs upwards of $10, it has never been more important to see a movie for little to no money. If you have ever been among the throngs of people camped out on the National Mall on a summer Monday evening, you know what I mean. The National Mall is only the beginning of the cheap cinema offers in the D.C. area. From outdoor screenings under the stars in the summer to movie nights at museums, embassies, bars, libraries, and even theaters throughout the year, here is your list of where to go to get your fix of free flicks.

YEAR-ROUND SCREENINGS

American City Diner
5532 Connecticut Ave., NW (at Morrison Street)
(202) 244-1949
www.americancitydiner.com
Every night at 8 p.m.

The Catch You are going to be tempted to order a shake and fries.

Catch a classic movie from the 1940s, '50s, or '60s every night of the week at this classic train-car diner. From *The Jazz Singer* to *The Graduate,* the American City Diner also occasionally sneaks in more recent films as well. Head back to the "Movie Deck," an enclosed patio with a screen, and grab a seat at one of the tables. This is a busy diner so expect to order something, but you can slip by with a cup of coffee, just $1.95 with free refills.

Busboys and Poets
2021 14th St., NW (at V Street); (202) 387-7638
1025 5th St., NW (at K Street); (202) 789-2227
4251 South Campbell Ave. (Shirlington Village), Arlington, VA; (703) 379-9757
www.busboysandpoets.com
Sundays at 8 p.m. (14th & V)
Saturdays at 11 p.m. (5th & K)
Sundays at 9 p.m. (Shirlington)

Free Movies by the Week

(Year-Round)

TIME	MONDAY	TUESDAY	WEDNESDAY	THURSDAY	FRIDAY	SATURDAY	SUNDAY
Various Times						National Gallery	National Gallery
Noon		National Geographic (spring & fall)					
2 p.m.							Freer Gallery
6:30 p.m.			Japan Culture Center (3rd Wednesday)		Embassy of Argentina (twice a month)		Japan Cultural Center (last Friday)
7 p.m.		Library of Congress	Library of Congress	Library of Congress	Library of Congress Freer Gallery		
8 p.m.	American City Diner	American City Diner / Washington Psychotronic Film Society	American City Diner	American City Diner / Hirshhorn Museum	American City Diner	American City Diner	American City Diner / Busboys & Poets (14th & V) / EatBar
9 p.m.							Busboys & Poets (Shirlington)
11 p.m.						Busboys & Poets (5th & K)	

(Summer)

TIME	MONDAY	TUESDAY	WEDNESDAY	THURSDAY	FRIDAY	SATURDAY	SUNDAY
6:30 p.m.	National Theatre			Family Movie Night	Family Movie Night	Family Movie Night	
Nightfall	Crystal Screen / Screen on the Green		Dupont Movie Mania (last Wednesday) / NoMa Film Festival	Riverfront Reels	Rosslyn Film Festival	Rockville Town Square	Family Movie Night

The best left-leaning restaurant/bookshop/coffeehouse/fair-trade market/ concert hall/poetry space/movie theater in town, Busboys and Poets is a popular watering hole for those who want to discuss social justice and peace or enjoy poetry, music, or readings. Every week the Focus In! film series presents films that explore provocative subjects such as the environment, civil rights, GLBT issues, and politics, followed by discussions with many of the filmmakers. Screenings take place at all three locations; Sundays at 8 p.m. at 14th & V, Sundays at 9 p.m. in Shirlington, and Saturdays at 11 p.m. at 5th and K. Be sure to check the schedule for additional monthly screenings, including the Community Cinema, which presents films from the PBS documentary series Independent Lens.

Docs In Progress
GWU's Media and Public Affairs Building
Lower Level Auditorium (B-07)
805 21st St., NW (corner of 21st and H Streets)
(301) 789-2797
www.docsinprogress.org
The Catch $5 Suggested Donation

A bimonthly series of unfinished documentaries, including a lively feedback session with the filmmakers. Docs In Progress also teaches classes in film production, which can be taken for free or at a greatly reduced price if you work as a volunteer with the organization.

EatBar
2761 Washington Blvd. (at North Daniel Street)
Arlington, VA
(703) 778-5051
www.tallularestaurant.com
www.myspace.com/eatbar
Sundays at 8 p.m.

A casual pub with a dash of style in Arlington, Eatbar hosts a fun assortment of films ranging from Sing-a-Long-a *Sound of Music* to an all-day Bill Murray festival. The crowd can get boisterous, so if you're a stickler for dead silence when you watch movies, this may not be the place for you. Eatbar provides free movie candy and popcorn with white truffles (see what I mean about a dash of style?). And if you're inclined to have a drink or dinner, the menu of fresh bar goodies is pretty reasonably priced.

Embassy of Argentina

1600 New Hampshire Ave., NW (at Q Street)
(202) 238-6464
www.embassyofargentina.us/en/home/news.htm
Fridays at 6:30 p.m. (about twice a month)

The Embassy of Argentina hosts free films from that South American nation, but you need to make a reservation via e-mail at least four days before each screening. E-mail subscribers will also be alerted to other events at the embassy, including free tango classes.

Freer Gallery of Art

1150 Jefferson Dr., SW (at 12th Street)
(202) 633-1000
www.asia.si.edu
Fridays at 7 p.m.
Sundays at 2 p.m.

Along with neighboring Sackler Gallery, the Freer Gallery of Art houses the National Museum of Asian Art, and that extends into the film selections. Throughout the year, the curators host in-depth retrospectives of new and classic films from Japan, Korea, China, Iran, India, and elsewhere in Asia. Most screenings take place on Friday at 7 p.m. or Sunday at 2 p.m.; additional screenings occur during the week.

Goddard Space Flight Center's Visitor Center

ICESat Road and Greenbelt Road (SR 193)
(301) 286-3978
www.nasa.gov/centers/goddard/visitor

The NASA folks show family-friendly space-themed features and documentaries on periodic Saturdays.

Hirshhorn Museum and Sculpture Garden

Independence Avenue and 7th Street SW
(202) 633-1000
www.hirshhorn.si.edu
Thursdays at 8 p.m.

The Smithsonian home for modern and contemporary art presents independent films and documentaries about many of the artists featured in the galleries. Check out the regular schedule of talks with film artists on Thursday evenings at 8 p.m., as well as other talks, tours, and activities for young artists.

Historical Society of Washington

801 K St., NW (at Mount Vernon Square)
(202) 383-1850
www.historydc.org
Saturdays at 2 p.m. (once or twice a month)

The Historical Society schedules films every month, coordinated with an exhibition in their gallery. Hip Hop Cinema, a series of documentaries about hip-hop and hip-hop culture accompanied by a live performance, takes place on Saturday afternoons once or twice a month at 2 p.m.

The Hoff Theater at University of Maryland

Stamp Student Union
Campus Drive and Union Lane
College Park, MD
(301) 405-0569
www.union.umd.edu/hoff
www.see.umd.edu
freestuff.umd.edu

The Hoff Theater at the Stamp Student Union at the University of Maryland looks and feels like any other mall movie theater but with one big difference—about half the movies are free. Although the first-run Hollywood hits and independent films aren't free, a number of academic departments, student organizations, and outside groups sponsor free screenings of foreign films, documentaries, classics, and blockbusters. All screenings are open to the public.

Play a Part

The **D.C. Film Alliance** is the ultimate clearing house for film information in the Washington area. The organization coordinates many of the more than 50 film festivals in the area every year, as well as spreads the word about screenings, workshops, gatherings, casting, and crew calls in the region. Volunteering for any of the area film festivals is not only a great way to network and get more film savvy, but it also gets you into the festival screenings and parties for free, not to mention festival swag. Also be sure to check out the **D.C. Film Salon,** a quarterly gathering of local filmmakers and others who meet to discuss current projects, screen dailies of works in progress, and exchange ideas. (202) 393-4266; www.dcfilm.org

Inter-American Development Bank Cultural Center

1300 New York Ave. (between 13th and 14th Streets)
(202) 623-3774
www.iadb.org/cultural

And you thought the only thing creative about banks was their accounting. The Inter-American Development Bank (IDB) assists developing countries in Latin America and the Caribbean and uses its cultural center to promote the artists in those countries. To develop a wider audience, the Center holds cultural events such as film premieres twice monthly.

Japan Information and Culture Center

1155 21st St., NW (between L and M Streets)
(202) 238-6949
www.us.emb-japan.go.jp/jicc/index.htm
www.dcanimeclub.org
Third Wednesday at 6:30 p.m. (J Film Series)
Last Friday at 6:30 p.m. (Anime Series)

The cultural arm of the Japanese Embassy, the Japan Information and Culture Center covers the gamut of Japanese film and animation with its two series of screenings. On the third Wednesday of every month, the J Film Series showcases full-length films. On the last Friday of the month, the center hosts the D.C. Anime Club for aficionados of Japanese cartoons. Don't be surprised to see more than a few people in costume (please leave your anime weapons at home). Reservations required.

The Library of Congress

101 Independence Ave., SE (between 1st and South Capitol Streets)
(202) 707-5000 (general information)
(202) 707-5677 (Pickford Theater reservation line)
www.loc.gov/pickford
Tuesdays to Fridays at 7 p.m.

You think you have a hard time deciding among one hundred cable TV channels, but the curators at the Library of Congress have it much harder. They have to choose one film a day from more than a million movies and videos. Each year they choose several themes or subjects (Abraham Lincoln, Bob Hope and American Film Comedy, Blaxploitation Films, Jazz on Film, etc.) and program a diverse schedule of films and television shows around them. Screenings take place Tuesday through Friday evenings at 7. The intimate theater only seats sixty, so call a week ahead to reserve your spot or try your luck on the standby line. The Library of Congress occasionally has screenings in other venues in the complex.

National Archives

700 Constitution Ave. NW (between 7th and 9th Streets)
(202) 357-5000
www.archives.gov/nae

During the day, the McGowan Theater runs two short films on a continuous loop about the National Archives and the priceless documents it houses. At night it shows a variety of important feature documentaries and independent films that might not make it to the big screen anywhere else. One of the highlights of the year is the chance to view every documentary that's up for an Oscar that year, both feature and short subject. On other nights, the theater is occupied with weighty lectures and panel discussions. Admission is first come, first served, and doors open thirty minutes before show time.

Busting Blockbuster

Forget about spending more than $5 to rent a DVD at Blockbuster or that $15-a-month Netflix membership fee. Most local libraries have a large collection of DVDs for loan, from documentaries to Hollywood hits to independent films to TV shows. You will find plenty on the shelves to please all tastes. You can borrow a DVD for up to three weeks, but watch out for the $1-per-day late fee.

National Gallery of Art

4th and Constitution Avenue, NW (between 3rd and 9th Streets)
(202) 737-4215
www.nga.gov
Saturdays and Sundays at various times, plus other screenings during the week

In addition to the Raphaels, Cezannes, and Van Goghs that line the wall of the National Gallery, every winter, spring, and summer the curators put together four to six in-depth retrospectives of different film artists, genres, countries, or themes. Recent series included The Rebel Set: Film and the Beat Legacy, Afghanistan on Film, Michelangelo Antonioni: The Italian Treasures, England's New Wave, 1958–1964, Aaron Copland: Music for American Movies, and Edward Hopper and American Movie Culture. Multiple screenings are held on Saturday and Sunday and often on weekdays as well. Seating is on a first-come, first-served basis.

National Geographic Museum
1145 17th St., NW (at M Street)
(202) 857-7588
www.ngmuseum.org
Tuesdays at noon (spring and fall)

Every Tuesday at lunchtime, instead of grabbing some fast food and grousing about your job, take a journey to a far-off land or explore an age-old culture at the National Geographic Museum's free documentary film screenings.

National Library of Medicine
Lister Hill Auditorium, Building 38A (on the NIH Campus)
8600 Rockville Pike
(301) 594-5983
www.nlm.nih.gov

The National Library of Medicine often screens films to coincide with its exhibitions. Don't expect to just see *M.A.S.H.* or *Patch Adams.* For an exhibit about the history of forensics, the museum hosted a series of murder mysteries including those of Sherlock Holmes and Tim Burton's *Sleepy Hollow.* And the movie snacks are on the house.

National Museum of the American Indian
Fourth Street & Independence Avenue, SW
(202) 633-1000
www.nmai.si.edu

Along with an array of free performances, workshops, talks, and tours, the National Museum of the American Indian also showcases films by or about Native Americans. Each month, the curators choose a new film for their daily screening. Films run the gamut, from award-winning independent feature films to short documentaries. Screenings take place at least once a day but are sometimes repeated throughout the day, with occasional evening screens.

The Washington Psychotronic Film Society

The Warehouse
1021 7th St., NW (between K and L Streets)
(202) 736-1732
www.wpfs.org
Tuesdays at 8 p.m.

The Catch Screenings are free, but a $2 donation is appreciated.

Devotees of psychotronic films (loosely defined as not your normal flick) get together every Tuesday evening to revel in a collection of obscure, off-the-beaten-track, sometimes trashy, sometimes artsy films. From experimental films to student films to long-lost trashy slashers, the Washington Psychotronic Film Society will find it and show it. Evenings are hosted by Dr. Schlock, who promises "rare eye-candy and groovy tunes" before the screenings and "cheap prizes" after.

Everyone's a Critic

Here is your chance to let Hollywood know what you think of its movies. Many major film studios run private screenings of soon-to-be-released films to gauge public opinion and to determine how to market said films. Film Metro's Web site is a clearinghouse for many of the previews available around the country, including those in D.C. Just register for free, and you will have access to a schedule of previews taking place during the next two weeks. If tickets are available for a movie you are interested in, click on it and print the ticket. Tickets are usually only available two days before a scheduled screening, and they go fast, so plan ahead. Beware that Film Metro distributes more tickets than there are seats in a theater, to ensure a full house for every screening. Make sure you arrive early. www.filmmetro.com

A few other sites post free screenings and contests for movie passes nationwide:

www.freemoviescreenings.net
www.ew.com/ew/freescreening
www.wildaboutmovies.com/screenings

BETTER THAN THE BOOK:
MOVIES AT PUBLIC LIBRARIES

Washington, D.C., Public Library

Anacostia (Interim) Library
1800 Good Hope Rd., SE (at 18th Street)
(202) 715-7707
www.dclibrary.org

Martin Luther King Jr. Memorial Library, Central Library
901 G St., NW (at 9th Street)
(202) 727-0321
www.dclibrary.org

On most Monday, Tuesday, and Thursday nights, one or both of these Washington public library branches host screenings of popular films.

Arlington County Public Library

Central Library
1015 North Quincy St. (at 10th Street North)
(703) 228-5990 (main)
www.arlingtonva.us/lib

Cross-cultural documentaries and foreign films are shown on the 3rd Thursday of the month, followed by a group discussion.

Shirlington Branch Library
4200 Campbell Ave. (in Shirlington Village)
(703) 228-6545
http://shirlingtonlibrary.wordpress.com
www.arlingtonva.us/lib

The Shirlington Branch Library has a regular schedule of films every month: family films on the 1st and 3rd Sunday at 2 p.m.; Hollywood musicals on the 2nd Monday at 7 p.m.; themed films on the 1st and 3rd Tuesday of the month at 7 p.m.; documentaries on selected Saturday afternoons.

Montgomery County Public Library

Aspen Hill
4407 Aspen Hill Rd. (between Parkland and Marriana Drives)
Rockville, MD
(240) 773-9410
www.montgomerycountymd.gov/library

The Montgomery Country Public Library programs batches of films in festivals throughout the year (mysteries, foreign films, etc.)

SUMMER SCREENINGS

Once the summer rolls around, forget about forking over cash to see a movie. Spread a blanket in a park and watch a movie under the stars; you'd be hard pressed to find a patch of green or public space at which movies aren't shown. Many film festivals run all summer long, with a handful taking place during a shorter time. In addition to movies, many of the events also include pre-show concerts, performances and activities for children, as well as free popcorn and other giveaways.

Throughout the Summer

Crystal Screen Outdoor Film Festival: 18th and Bell Street, Crystal City, VA; (703) 412-9430; www.crystalcity.org; Crystal Screen wins the prize for being the area's most extensive festival. Each year, the organizers choose a theme (James Bond, Superheroes, etc.) and run more than twenty weeks' worth of classics and recent hits. Enjoy the free popcorn and cotton candy, as well as fun activities before the show. Every Monday night from May through September.

Dupont Movie Mania: Stead Park, 1625 P St., NW, at 16th Street; (202) 491-1275; www.reishmangroup.com; last Wednesday of each month from June to August.

Family Movie Night: Various recreation centers around D.C.; (202) 698-2205; www.dpr.dc.gov; family movies screened under the stars at various

D.C. parks and recreation centers every Thursday to Sunday night from late June to late September.

Movies on the Lawn: Manassas Museum, 9101 Prince William St. (between Main and Liberty Streets), Manassas, VA; (703) 368-1873; www.manassas museum.org; on select Friday nights from June to August, the Manassas Museum screens classic movies from the 1950s or '60s.

The National Theatre Summer Cinema: 1321 Pennsylvania Ave. (between 13th and 14th Streets); (202) 783-3372; www.nationaltheatre.org; a plethora of film classics, independent films, and Hollywood blockbusters are shown every Monday night at 6:30 p.m. Tickets are distributed on a first-come, first-served basis at 6 p.m. Limit one ticket per person.

NoMa Outdoor Film Festival: 2nd and K Streets, NW; (202) 289-0111; www .nomabid.org; classic films and recent hits that fit the bill under the film festival's yearly theme. Free popcorn and music. Every Wednesday from June through August.

Riverfront Reels: New Jersey Avenue, NE, and Tingey Street; (202) 465-7093; www.capitolriverfront.org; theme festival with fun pre-show events and giveaways. Every Thursday night from June to August.

Rockville Town Square Outdoor Movies: Town Square between Maryland Avenue and Gibbs Street; (301) 998-8178; www.rockvilletownsquare.com; recent hits and family favorites on Saturday nights from May to July.

Rosslyn Outdoor Film Festival: Gateway Park at Lee Highway near Key Bridge; (703) 276-7759; www.rosslynva.org; classic films and recent hits linked by a theme with fun pre-show activities. Every Friday night from May to September.

Screen on the Green: National Mall between 4th and 7th Streets; (877) 262-5866; www.nps.gov/archive/ncro/PublicAffairs/MonthlyCalendar.htm; this is the godfather of all D.C. outdoor screenings. Big crowds spread out on the Mall and enjoy an eclectic mix of recent hits, classics, and kitschy flicks. Monday nights, July and August.

June

Cox Movies under the Moon: Van Dyck Park, 3730 Old Lee Hwy. (between Old Post Road and Layton Hall Drive), Fairfax, VA; (703) 480-5241; www.moviesunderthemoon.com; recent family hits. The last week of June.

July

Alexandria Outdoor Film Festival: Ben Brenman Park: 500 Duke St.; Alexandria, VA; (703) 883-4686; www.alexandriafilmfest.com; two or three family-friendly movies over one weekend in July.

Bethesda Outdoor Movies: Stars on the Avenue: Woodmont Triangle at the corner of Norfolk and Auburn Avenues, Bethesda, MD; www.bethesda.org; (301) 215-6660; a mix of family films, documentaries, and recent hits. The last week in July.

August

Starlight Cinema: 585 Trinity Parkway off US 29, Centreville, VA; (703) 324-7469; (703) 324-7469 (rain cancellation info); www.fairfaxcounty.gov/parks/performances/starlight.htm; drive-in movies for the whole family, with pre-show entertainment and activities for kids. Every Saturday night in August.

Strathmore NIH Outdoor Film Festival: Strathmore Music Center, 5301 Tuckerman Lane, North Bethesda, MD; (301) 581-5100; www.filmfestnih.org; a ten-day festival of classics, family films, and recent hits, with fun activities for the kids before the screening. Mid-August.

COMEDY:
CHEAP JOKES

"I've been asked to say a couple of words about my husband, Fang.
"How about 'short' and 'cheap'?"
—PHYLLIS DILLER

Washington isn't known as a comedy town, and with good reason. Besides the political gaffes and scandals, there isn't a lot to laugh at here. A few clubs, such as the Improv and Warner Theater, showcase top-name comedians, but the cost of giggles at those places is no laughing matter. Seriously, once you pay the hefty cover charge and then shell out more money for overpriced drinks, you'll feel as if the joke's on you. You can have the last laugh by skipping the pricey clubs and checking out free comedy nights at smaller venues. Most feature stand-up newcomers or more established comics practicing new material. The schedules do change from time to time, so be sure to call ahead to confirm information.

The Bethesda Theater
7719 Wisconsin Ave. (at Cheltenham Street)
Bethesda, MD
(301) 657-7827
usher@bethesdatheater.com
www.bethesdatheater.com

The Catch Become a volunteer usher to see the shows for free.

Every Friday and Saturday evening after their main stage show, The Bethesda Theater hosts a late-night comedy and cabaret performance. You can see the show for free as a volunteer usher. Make a full night of it by ushering at both shows. E-mail the theater a week or two in advance to reserve an ushering slot.

The Bureau
University of Maryland
Stamp Student Union
Campus Drive and Union Lane
College Park, MD
www.umdbureau.com

This all-purpose campus comedy troupe performs sketch, stand-up, and improv comedy, as well as music, once or twice a month.

Palace of Wonders
1210 H St. NE (between 12th and 13th Streets)
(202) 398-7469
www.palaceofwonders.com

Titter Tryouts: Stand-Up Open Mics

An entire underground culture of closeted comedians exists in D.C. Lawyers, lobbyists, government workers, engineers, and computer geeks take to the stage at the many stand-up open-mic nights in the region. These evenings are a mix of newbies and more seasoned funnymen, so be prepared for a few groaners mixed in with the belly laughs. If you're ready to have your moment in the spotlight, just show up early. These open mics are free with no cover or minimum.

All Stars Comedy Club, 2317 Wilson Blvd. (at Curtis Road), Arlington, VA; (703) 739-7377; www.allstarscomedy.com: Tuesdays and Wednesdays at 8:30 p.m.

Solly's Tavern, 1942 11th St., NW (at U Street), (202) 232-6590; www.sollystavern.com; Tuesdays at 8 p.m.

JoJo Restaurant & Bar, 1518 U St., NW (at North 15th Street), (202) 319-9350; www.jojorestandbar.com; Tuesdays at 9 p.m.

Ri-Ra Irish Pub, 2915 Wilson Blvd. (at North Fillmore Street), Arlington, VA; (703) 248-9888; www.standupcomedytogo.com; www.rira.com; Wednesdays at 8 p.m.

Mad Hatter, 1831 M St., NW (between 18th and 19th Streets); (202) 833-1495; www.madhatterdc.com; Tuesdays at 9 p.m.

The Comedy Spot, Ballston Common Mall; 4238 Wilson Blvd.; Arlington, VA; (703) 294-5233; www.comedyindc.com; Thursdays at 7:30 p.m.

Topaz Hotel, 1733 N St., NW (off Dupont Circle); (202) 393-3000; www.topazhotel.com; www.standupcomedytogo.com; Thursdays at 8 p.m.

Best Western Capitol Skyline, 10 I St., SW (at South Capitol Street); (202) 488-7500; www.capitolskyline.com; Fridays at 8 p.m.

Arlington Cinema & Drafthouse, 2903 Columbia Pike (off South Walter Reed Drive), Arlington, VA; (703) 486-2345; www.arlingtondrafthouse.com; Saturdays at 10:30 p.m.

The Palace of Wonders is D.C.'s, and maybe the world's, only vaudeville the-ater–sideshow museum with a full bar. The Palace hosts an open-mic comedy night on Sunday evenings and one for magicians, jugglers, solo musicians, vaudeville performers, and comedians on Tuesdays. Both shows are free, but they do charge for other shows during the week.

Washington Improv Theater
1835 14th St., NW (at P Street)
(202) 204-7770
www.washingtonimprovtheater.com

The Catch *Volunteer or usher for free performances or classes.*

The Washington Improv Theater is D.C.'s professional, home-grown improv troupe. The company is made up of different ensembles that produce their own shows, ranging from brainy and edgy to goofy and zany. You can slip into the shows for free by becoming a volunteer usher. WIT also runs an extensive program of classes in improv, and you sit in on free classes after volunteering for forty-eight hours. Volunteers assist the staff by usher-ing and doing administrative work. The theater also runs free introductory workshops four times a year.

DANCE:
FREE EXPRESSION

"Dancing: the highest intelligence
in the freest body."
—ISADORA DUNCAN

While D.C. may be best known for its politicians' skill at dancing around the truth, the little-known truth is that there is a lot of actual dancing in the region. Whether you are serious about learning the basics of ballet, jazz, or tap or want to strut your stuff on the ballroom floor, you can find a class, club, or studio to get you on your feet, if you're willing to pitch in around the studio a few hours a week. Some restaurants, clubs, embassies, and the public library also host a number of free classes.

BalletNOVA Center for Dance
3443 Carlin Springs Rd. (at Columbia Pike)
Falls Church, VA
(703) 778-3008
www.centerdancecompany.org

The Catch Work the front desk for free classes. The math: one hour of work = $14 toward classes

The BalletNOVA Center for Dance offers an extensive schedule of classes for the novice to the professional. Ballet gets the bulk of classes, but jazz, tap, modern, and hip-hop are taught as well. A limited number of volunteer positions exist, but if you get a spot, one hour of work at the front desk counts as $14 towards classes, and the classes run about $17 apiece.

CityDance Ensemble at Strathmore
5301 Tuckerman Lane (at Rockville Pike)
North Bethesda, MD
(301) 581-5204
www.citydance.net

The Catch Volunteer four to six hours a week in exchange for free classes.

One of D.C.'s most admired modern dance companies offers classes in all forms of dance, including ballet, modern, tap, hip-hop, and ballroom, as well as yoga, tai chi, and Pilates classes. You can take an unlimited number of free classes if you join the ensemble's work-study program. The program is open to anyone willing to make a one-year commitment to work one four- to six-hour shift a week at the front desk answering phones or greeting students. You can also volunteer on a less frequent basis or barter your services for free classes. The deal you strike depends on your skills or the time you can put in.

Work-study students and volunteers can get comps to company performances. Get a sneak peak at new works the company is developing at its informal gatherings called CityDance 360, which take place once or twice a month. Enjoy the free wine and cheese, too.

Dance Place
3225 8th St., NE (at Kearny Street)
(202) 269-1600
www.danceplace.org

The Catch Work-study students must work approximately twelve hours a month in exchange for unlimited free classes but have to pay for their first four classes.

Dance Place specializes in modern and African dance, with the occasional belly dance class thrown in for good measure. Work-study students can take unlimited free classes in exchange for a six-month commitment to help out around the office, school, or studios. Depending on the assignment you accept, you will be expected to put in about twelve hours a month. Before joining the work-study corps, you have to pay for your first four classes.

Elan Dancesport Center
8442 Lee Hwy.
Fairfax, VA
(703) 289-3070
www.elandancesport1.com

The Catch Work one five- to seven-hour shift a week for free unlimited classes.

If you can't get enough of *Dancing with the Stars,* this is the place for you. Elan teaches swing, salsa, tango, and every other kind of partner dance you've ever heard of and a few that only your grandparents know. Volunteers can take unlimited "studio" classes (only those taught by Elan staff members) in exchange for working one five- to seven-hour front desk shift a week. You must make a commitment of at least two months to participate.

Embassy of Argentina
1600 New Hampshire Ave., NW
(202) 238-6464
www.embassyofargentina.us/en/home/news.htm

Dance Is the Answer

Dance Is the Answer is a dance festival that runs for about ten days at the end of April, and it's a Cheap Bastard's dream come true. During that time, most dance studios, companies, and artists offer free classes, workshops, lectures, open rehearsals, and performances in every style of dance. The ten days are jammed with opportunities to experience everything from Indian dance performances to tap dance classes, from an open rehearsal at Step Afrika! to modern dance master classes. A few events are ticketed, but the vast majority are free. To find out more about Dance Is the Answer, go to its Web site: www.danceistheanswer.org.

Who better to learn the tango from than the country that invented it? The Embassy of Argentina offers a free six-week introduction-to-tango workshop several times throughout the year. The classes are popular, so register for the class online.

Habana Village

1834 Columbia Rd., NW
(202) 462-6310
www.habanavillage.com

The Catch Cover on Friday and Saturday nights, free on Wednesday and Thursday.

This is the best place to head to in D.C. if you want to experience a little bit of old Cuba. The salsa music is hot, and the mojitos are tasty but pricey. Wednesday and Thursday nights are free, so enjoy the salsa dancing starting at 9 p.m. From 7:30 to 9:30 p.m. Habana Village runs salsa classes, although it costs $10 to participate. Friday and Saturday nights see live music and big crowds and a $6 cover charge.

The Jam Cellar

Josephine Butler Parks Center
2437 Fifteenth St., NW (between Chapin and Euclid Streets)
(202) 558-0338
www.thejamcellar.com

Swing down to the gorgeous Josephine Butler Parks Center, a restored 18th century mansion, for beginner jitterbug lessons every Tuesday night at 9 p.m. After the lessons, stay for the dance party, which is only $6 per person.

Joy of Motion
Atlas Performing Arts Center, 1333 H St., NE (off Linden Place); (202) 399-6763
Dupont Circle, 1643 Connecticut Ave., NW (at Hilyer Place); (202) 387-0911
Friendship Heights, 5207 Wisconsin Ave., NW (at Harrison Street), (202) 362-3042
Bethesda, 7315 Wisconsin Ave., Suite 180E (at Elm Street); (301) 986-0016

The Catch Work one office shift a week or help at two performances a month for free classes.

The four Joy of Motion locations offer classes in jazz, ballet, modern, and tap, as well as anything from flamenco to African-Caribbean to tribal belly dance to Persian to yoga. A number of different work-study opportunities are available. Choose to work one shift a week in their main office doing light administrative duties or pitch in backstage at two performances a month in exchange for free, unlimited, regularly scheduled classes and get a 20 percent discount on performance classes and workshops.

Lima Restaurant and Lounge
1401 K St., NW (at 14th Street)
(202) 789-2800
www.limarestaurant.com

The Catch No cover on Monday nights but a steep cover the rest of the week.

Lima is a popular, swanky Latin-inspired restaurant and lounge that plays mostly house and hip-hop. Usually, one has to pay his or her way into this club, but it's free on Latin night. Start off the evening with a free beginner or intermediate salsa class from 9 to 10:30 p.m. And if the free class isn't enough for you, ladies even drink free from 9 to 11 p.m.

Lucky Bar
1221 Connecticut Ave., NW (between N and M Streets)
(202) 332-3733
www.luckybardc.com

On Monday nights, this sports bar/dive bar/burger joint with a frat house feel turns international with its popular salsa night. Free dance lessons beginning at 8 p.m.

McGinty's Public House
911 Ellsworth Dr. (between Fenton Street and Georgia Avenue)
Silver Spring, MD
www.mcgintyspublichouse.com

Swing every Sunday at McGinty's. From 6 to 8 p.m., the bar hosts swing classes for a charge, but from 8 p.m. on anyone can grab a partner and swing the night away.

Mezè

2437 18th St., NW (between North Adams Mill Road & North Belmont Road)
(202) 797-0017
www.mezedc.com

This Turkish restaurant and lounge may give you a bellyache, but it has nothing to do with the food. Every Sunday night at 10 p.m., Mezè holds a free belly dance class.

West End Neighborhood Library

1101 24th St., NW (at L Street)
(202) 724-8707
www.dclibrary.org

Put a rose in your mouth and head down to the library every Saturday afternoon for a free tango lesson. The session runs from 2:30 to about 5 p.m.; no partner or experience required.

FOOD:
ON THE HOUSE

*"I know how hard it is for you
to put food on your family."*
— GEORGE W. BUSH

Fast food, gourmet food, exotic food, health food, breads, cakes, wings, hors d'oeuvres . . . Anything you desire, you can find it in D.C. But for free? Yes, you can. Wander through gourmet markets, high-end supermarkets, and selected specialty stores around the city and you will find a delightful (and filling) selection of samples to chow down on. Make your way to a number of bars and restaurants that set out some grand and some not-so-grand spreads during Happy Hour.

HAPPY HOURS & BUFFETS

Many bars, pubs, clubs, and restaurants around the area offer some kind of free food during happy hour. What you'll find runs the gamut from basic bar food (wings and potato skins) to sumptuous buffets (Middle Eastern, Latin, etc.) to fine dining. Usually, you're expected to buy a drink first, but happy hour is known for its drink discounts. If you don't drink, or don't feel like footing the bill for a martini, just order a club soda. Be sure to leave the bartender a nice tip. Yes, even Cheap Bastards should remember to tip. While I have only included those places that have a long history of offering free eats, always call ahead to confirm, as policies change over time.

WASHINGTON

Capitol Hill

Hawk 'n' Dove
329 Pennsylvania Ave., SE (between 3rd and 4th Streets)
(202) 543-3553
www.hawkanddoveonline.com

You're likely to hear Capitol Hill staffers grousing about their bosses on the next bar stool at this iconic dive. Underpaid aides and interns are drawn by the bar's cheap beer and free steak sandwiches or tacos during happy hour every Monday to Friday from 5 to 7 p.m.

Downtown

Bravo! Bravo!
1001 Connecticut Ave., NW (between K and L Street)
(202) 223-5330
www.bravobravodc.com

At happy hour, Bravo! Bravo! transitions from its daytime role as a somewhat nondescript restaurant serving up burgers, sandwiches, and salads to a
popular salsa club. To ease the transition, when the kitchen closes at 5 p.m.,
the owners set up a small buffet of free bar food (meatballs, wings, fries).
Monday to Friday.

Ceiba Restaurant
701 14th St., NW (at G Street)
(202) 393-3983
www.ceibarestaurant.com

This stylish Latin restaurant is a popular destination for the after-work
crowd. During happy hour, it offers up tasty Peruvian ceviche, mini Cuban
sandwiches and guacamole with tomatillos. The snacks are available at the
bar from 4 to 7 p.m. and 9:30 to 11 p.m. every Monday to Friday along with
$5 drink and appetizer specials.

Equinox Restaurant
818 Connecticut Ave., NW (between H and I Streets)
(202) 331-8118
www.equinoxrestaurant.com

This is one happy hour you might think about putting your tie on for.
Equinox is located a block away from the White House and is a favorite of
politicos and visiting celebrities. A few days before the inauguration, the
Obamas celebrated Michelle's 45th birthday here. The restaurant is considered
to be one of the finest in D.C., so you're not going to be chowing down on
buffalo wings and pot stickers here. Every Friday from 5 to 7 p.m., chef Todd
Gray prepares delectable seasonal canapés. The drinks can be pricey, but
where else can you rub elbows with a senator over duck quesadillas with
cherry coulis?

Lima Restaurant and Lounge
1401 K St. (at 14th Street, NW)
(202) 789-2800
www.limarestaurant.com

Swanky and stylish restaurant/lounge brings in a buttoned-up K Street crowd to loosen up for an extended happy hour Monday to Friday. Happy hour specials run from 4 to 9 p.m., but the most appetizing fare—empanadas, chicken croquettes, and tamales—comes out from 5 to 7:30 p.m. The downstairs lounge hosts an open bar from 5 to 6 p.m.

Town and Country Lounge
Mayflower Hotel
1127 Connecticut Ave. (at Desales Street, NW)
(202) 347-3000

The dark wood and deep leather of this historic bar has seen its fair share of spies, power brokers, high-priced prostitutes, and presidents. The Mayflower Hotel has played an integral part in many unforgettable scandals (Marion Barry smoked crack here, Eliot Spitzer trysted here, and Monica Lewinsky spilled her guts here). What's the draw? It could be the free wings and pub grub during happy hour. Be warned: drinks are pricey, but then again, it's nothing compared to what that gal sitting next to you may be charging.

Dupont Circle

Vidalia Restaurant
1990 M St., NW (at 20th Street)
(202) 659-1990
www.vidaliadc.com

One usually has to lay down a pretty penny to dine at Vidalia, one of D.C.'s finest restaurants. But its happy hour is the time to snag some fine wine and mouthwatering hors d'oeuvres without needing even one penny. The restaurant's sommelier selects two or three of his favorite bottles for tastings Monday through Friday from 5:30 to 6:30 p.m. The wine is paired with some artfully prepared treats from the kitchen.

Foggy Bottom

The Exchange
1719 G St., NW (between 17th and 18th Streets)
(202) 393-4690
www.theexchangesaloon.com

Fridays from 5 to 7 p.m. dine on free spiced shrimp and cheese at this sports bar near the White House.

Friendship Heights

Bambule
5225 Wisconsin Ave., NW (at Ingomar Street)
Washington, D.C. 20015
(202) 966-0300

This tapas restaurant sets out some of their tasty little appetizers every weekday, 4 to 7 p.m.

Maggiano's Little Italy
5333 Wisconsin Ave., NW
(202) 966-5500
www.maggianos.com

Maggiano's Little Italy is a mega-restaurant that dishes out generous servings of pasta, bruschetta, and antipasti during happy hour, Tuesday to Fridays from 5 to 7 p.m.

ARLINGTON, VA

Bailey's Pub & Grille
Ballston Common Mall, 4238 Wilson Blvd. (at North Glebe Road);
(703) 465-1300

Aurora Highlands, 2010 Crystal Dr. (between 20th and 21st Streets South);
(703) 416-0452
Arlington, VA
www.tentcorp.com

Huge sports bars that offer tasty buffets of lasagna, fried chicken, etc. every
Wednesday night at 7 p.m.

The Bungalow
Alexandria, VA, 7003-C Manchester Blvd. (at Beulah Street); (703) 924-8730
Chantilly, VA, 13891 Metrotech Dr. (Lee Jackson Memorial Highway at Centerville Road); (703) 502-3925
Shirlington, VA, 2766 South Arlington Mill Dr. (at South Randolph Road);
(703) 578-0020
www.bungalow4u.com

Start the weekend off with a beach party. This Polynesian-themed bar offers
free wings, ravioli, meatballs, pizza, chips, and salsa on Fridays from 5 to 7
p.m.

La Tasca Spanish Restaurant
722 7th St., NW (between G and H Streets); (202) 347-9190
Arlington, VA, 2900 Wilson Blvd. (between North Fillmore and North Garfield
Streets); (703) 812-9120
www.latascausa.com

Lively Spanish restaurant featuring live music and flamenco performances.
Try the free paella every Friday at 6 p.m.

Piola
1550 Wilson Blvd. (between North Oak and North Pierce Streets)
Arlington, VA
(703) 528-1502
www.piola.it

Piola is an international pizza chain based in Italy with locations throughout
South America. This is its only D.C. offshoot. Known for its assortment of
creative and satisfying thin-crust pizzas, happy hour customers can sample
a pizza or two every weeknight from 4:30 to 8 p.m. If you want to try them
all, don't eat for a week and show up on Sunday night when all-you-can-eat
pizza is $15.

Sing for Your Supper

Check out these unusual places at which you can lend a hand or join the chanting to get yourself a healthy vegetarian meal.

Food Not Bombs
Kay Spiritual Life Center
American University
4400 Massachusetts Ave., NW (at Nebraska Avenue)
(202) 885-3333
The Community Action & Social Justice office at American University serves up free vegetarian meals in Dupont Circle every Sunday at 3 p.m. as part of Food Not Bombs, an international organization that feeds hungry people as an act of protest against war and poverty. The meals are served up to anyone without restriction, although they are generally meant for the less fortunate among us. The organization could use extra hands to help prepare and distribute meals. Of course, volunteers are also well fed. Cooking begins at 1 p.m. on Sundays in the basement of Kay Spiritual Center.

Hare Krishna Temple
10310 Oaklyn Dr. (between Falls Road and Potomac Station Lane)
Potomac, MD
(301) 299-2100
The Hare Krishna Temple offers a free vegetarian feast every Sunday evening. Chanting begins at 5:30 p.m., and dining begins at 7:30 p.m. Everyone is welcome to attend this popular event at the main Krishna temple for the D.C. region. No need to shave your head.

FREE SAMPLES: **A SAMPLING**

D.C. has no shortage of gourmet and farmers' markets and specialty stores that overcharge for everything from a leg of lamb to olives. But these markets are gold mines for free samples. You can get a taste of almost anything from gourmet breads, cakes, and chocolates to olive oils, cheese, and exotic fruits.

Aji Ichiban

309 North Washington St. (between Hungerford Drive and Beall Avenue)
Rockville, MD
(301) 610-7798

This Asian candy store declares itself to be a "munchies paradise," but you won't find your run-of-the-mill chips and pretzels here. Instead, try some of the world's most unusual and intensely flavorful delicacies. You might think you're a contestant on *Survivor* when you get a look at items such as dried curry squid, mini roasted crabs, and preserved chili olives. Tamer selections do exist, such as chocolates, biscuits, and gummy candies, as well. Just about everything in the store is set out for sampling. The Rockville location is a bit out of the way but worth the drive.

Biagio Fine Chocolate

1904 18th St., NW (between T Street and Florida Avenue)
(202) 328-1506
www.biagiochocolate.com

Keep your eye out for this somewhat hidden Adams Morgan shop. Biagio Fine Chocolate offers samples of their delicious, exotic chocolates. A couple of times a month, small chocolate makers stop by the shop to show off their sweets, and customers can sit in on the tastings.

Co Co. Sala

929 F St., NW (between 9th and 10th Streets)
(202) 347-4265
www.cocosala.com

Indulge in artisanal chocolates at the Co Co. Sala boutique. Tastings run inconsistently—some days you might get to savor white chocolate with salt and pepper or dark chocolate with banana and ginger—but other days you might come up empty. Keep trying; it's worth the effort.

Cowgirl Creamery
919 F St., NW (between 9th and 10th Streets)
(202) 393-6880
www.cowgirlcreamery.com

Fromage fanatics can sample just about any cheese at Cowgirl Creamery. Try any of the house brand cheese or the ones displayed by the register. Come back on Thursday afternoons from 4 to 6 for a gourmet beer or wine tasting.

Creative Cakes
8814 Brookville Rd.
Silver Spring, MD
(301) 587-1599
www.creativecakes.com

Once a month this wedding cake bakery opens its doors to let the public sample everything on the menu. Savor fifteen different cake flavors, with six different icings and fifteen different fillings. Try the white chiffon cake with crushed almond icing and raspberry filling or the red velvet cake with Swiss meringue chocolate buttercream icing and amaretto filling. The open houses are targeted at brides, but all are welcome. A wedding DJ spins tunes, making the experience a fun one. One Sunday a month from 12 to 3 p.m. You will need to register ahead.

Harris Teeter
Adams Morgan, 1631 Kalorama Rd., NW (at 17th Street); (202) 986-1415
South East, 1350 Potomac Ave., SE (between Pennsylvania Avenue and 12th Street); (202) 543-1040
North Bethesda, 11845 Old Georgetown Rd. (off Rockville Pike); (301) 468-3029
Pentagon Row, Arlington, VA, 900 Army Navy Dr. (between South Joyce and South Hayes Streets); (703) 413-7112
Ballston, Arlington, VA, 600 North Glebe Rd. (between North Carlin Springs Road and North Henderson Road); (703) 526-9100
Yorktown, Arlington, VA, 2425 North Harrison St. (at US 29); (703) 532-8663; www.harristeeter.com

Fresh from the Farm

Farmers' markets are not only one of the best sources for fresh, delicious, healthy, and locally grown fruits and vegetables, they are also a fantastic source of fresh, delicious, healthy, and locally grown samples! Walking from stall to stall during the more bountiful months, you can fill yourself up with samples of everything from heirloom tomatoes and organic apples to beans and peppers to fresh bread, cakes, and jams. More than sixty farmers' markets exist in the Washington area, most of them taking place during the warmer months, but a number of year-round markets exist in the area as well. Each has its own vibe.

Dupont Circle is fun, lively, and popular, a place to see and be seen. Takoma Park has a more Birkenstock/granola feel to it. RFK is a real no-nonsense market with many items in bulk. All have local vendors with yummy fruits and vegetables. Below is a listing of some of the more impressive markets, as well as resources for finding farmers' markets in other neighborhoods.

Dupont Circle FreshFarm Market, 20th and Q Streets, NW; (202) 362-8889; www.freshfarmmarkets.org
Sundays, 9 a.m. to 1 p.m., year-round
Eastern Market Outdoor Farmer's Market, 7th Street and North Carolina Avenue, SE; (202) 543-7293; www.easternmarketdc.com; Saturdays and Sundays, 7 a.m. to 4 p.m., year-round
Penn Quarter FreshFarm Market, 8th and D Streets, NW; (202) 362-8889; www.freshfarmmarkets.org; Thursdays, 3 to 7 p.m., April through December
RFK Stadium, Benning Road and Oklahoma Avenue, NE (parking lot No. 7); (301) 325-3762; Thursdays and Saturdays, 6 a.m. to 4:30 p.m. year-round unless there is a game at RFK
Takoma Park Farmer's Market, Laurel Avenue between Eastern and Carroll Avenues; (301) 422-0097; www.takomaparkmarket.com; Sundays, 10 a.m. to 2 p.m., year-round

Here are a few Web sites to search out other farmers' markets throughout the region:
http://apps.ams.usda.gov/FarmersMarkets
www.washingtonpost.com/farmersmarkets
www.freshfarmmarkets.org

This supermarket chain is a step up from your local Piggly Wiggly but not quite as hoity-toity as Whole Foods. Samples are always plentiful. Try their fresh breads and tapenades, cheeses, sandwich meats, and baked sweets, and if you are lucky enough, during the summer you can nab a generous sample of ice cream.

Rodman's

5100 Wisconsin Ave., NW (between Harrison and Garrison Streets)
(202) 363-3466
www.rodmans.com

A D.C. institution, Rodman's opened in 1955 as a humble corner drugstore and over the years has morphed into a discount international market selling exotic food, drinks, and housewares, as well as still filling prescriptions. The store sets out appetizing samples of breads, olive oils, cakes, cookies, and coffee. On Friday and Saturday, Rodman's hosts beer and wine tastings.

Super H Mart

Fairfax, VA, 10780 Lee Hwy. (between Meredith Drive and McLean Avenue);
(703) 273-0570
Silver Spring, MD, 12015 Georgia Ave. (between Shorefield Road and Henderson Avenue); (301) 942-5071
www.hmart.com

The ultimate destination for Asian food, these supermarkets have every Asian ingredient from curry sauces to udon noodles, plus a selection of chopsticks, rice cookers, and bamboo steamers. Drop by the stores on the weekends for samples of sushi and sashimi, kim chi, curries, soups, and other favorites.

Trader Joe's

Washington
Foggy Bottom, 1101 25th St., NW (between L and M Streets);
(202) 296-1921

Maryland
Chevy Chase, 6831 Wisconsin Ave. (off Bradley Boulevard);
(301) 907-0982
Rockville, 12268 Rockville Pike (north of Randolph Road);
(301) 468-6656

Silver Spring, 10741 Columbia Pike (between Crestmore and Hillwood Drives); (301) 681-1675

Virginia
Alexandria, 612 North Saint Asaph St. (between Wythe and Pendleton Streets); (703) 548-0611
Falls Church, 5847 Leesburg Pike (at Columbia Pike); (703) 379-5883
Falls Church, 7514 Leesburg Pike (at Pimmit Drive); (703) 288-0566
Fairfax, 9464 Main St. (at Picket Road); (703) 764-8550
www.traderjoes.com

You can always guarantee three things when you walk into any Trader Joe's: the staff will be sporting Hawaiian shirts; the staff will be having a good time; and the store will let you sample a plethora of items. Head toward the back of the store to try sizable samples of their house brand pizza, burritos, chips, and juices. Help yourself to a fresh cup of coffee, too.

The Westin Grand
2350 M St., NW (between 23rd and 24th Streets)
(202) 429-0100
www.starwoodhotels.com

Cushy hotel always has a bowl full of shiny apples available for the taking in the lobby.

Whole Foods

D.C.
Georgetown, 2323 Wisconsin Ave., NW (between Calvert Street and Observatory Lane); (202) 333-5393
Logan Circle, 1440 P St., NW (between 14th and 15th Streets); (202) 332-4300
Tenleytown, 4530 40th St., NW (between Brandywine and Albemarle Streets); (202) 237-5800

Maryland
Bethesda, 5269 River Rd. (between Brookside Road and Little Falls Parkway); (301) 984-4860
Silver Spring, 833 Wayne Ave. (between Fenton and Cedar Streets); (301) 608-9373
Rockville, 1649 Rockville Pike (between Congressional Lane and Halprine Road); (301) 984-4880

Virginia
Arlington, 2700 Wilson Blvd. (at North Danville Street); (703) 527-6596
Alexandria, 1700 Duke St. (at Holland Lane); (703) 706-0891

Fairfax, 4501 Market Commons Dr. (at Fair Lakes Parkway); (703) 222-2058
Falls Church, 7511 Leesburg Pike (between Evans Court and Pimmit Drive); (703) 448-1600
Reston, 11660 Plaza America Dr. (off Sunset Hills Road); (703) 736-0600
Vienna, 143 Maple Ave. East (at Mill Street NE); (703) 319-2000
www.wholefoodsmarket.com

This mega-healthy, natural, organic, and seriously pricey supermarket is a prime destination for samples. Most stores set out samples throughout the day, but a couple of local stores are the best bets for filling yourself up on tempting tidbits throughout the store. The Silver Spring and Falls Church stores have a number of weekly events featuring free samples. These usually take place Tuesday evenings and Wednesday afternoons and evenings at Silver Spring and Wednesday afternoons, Thursday evenings, and on weekends at both locations. All Whole Foods stores also have a schedule of classes, demonstrations, wine and beer tastings, and special events that are mostly all free.

WINE & BEER TASTINGS:
CHEAP DRUNK

*"I like best the wine drunk at the
cost of others."*
— BERGEN EVANS

Washington's wine shops and gourmet markets don't just allow you the chance to try some great wines, beers, and spirits from around the world; you can also learn a lot about the drinks as well. Stores in the city offer two types of tastings: Some local shops uncork a bottle or two for customers to try, hoping you'll buy. The more desirable situation is when a vintner or wine distributor offers an entire line of wines for the public to sample. You can also depend on their bringing something tasty along to cleanse the palate in between wines. Most shops offer a discount on whatever is being tasted that day, so if you're inspired to lay down some cash, this will lighten the blow.

The following listings are split between D.C. and Northern Virginia. There is a real dearth of wine shops and liquor stores in Montgomery County, which is surprising, considering it is one of the wealthiest counties in the country. The reason? The county liquor laws limit liquor store hours and impose extra taxes on bottles of hooch, making it hard for a shop to compete with shops in nearby D.C. or other counties.

Washington, D.C.: Tastings by the Week

	MONDAY	TUESDAY	WEDNESDAY	THURSDAY	FRIDAY	SATURDAY	SUNDAY
Afternoon					Magruder's Chevy Chase Wine	Bell Wine Chevy Chase Wine Circle Wine Cork & Fork (Bethesda) MacArthur Beverages Magruder's Pearson's Schneider's of Capitol Hill Wide World of Wines	
Evening	Vidalia Restaurant	Bistrot Lepic Vidalia Restaurant	Bell Wine Cleveland Park Wine Modern Liquors Vidalia Restaurant	Vidalia Restaurant	Cleveland Park Wine Vidalia Restaurant Wine Specialist	Cleveland Park Wine Wine Specialist	

WASHINGTON

Bell Wine & Spirits

1821 M St., NW (between 18th and 19th Streets)
(202) 223-4727
www.bellwineshop.com
Wednesdays, 6 to 8 p.m.
Saturdays, 1 to 5 p.m.

From the outside you might think this shop was just another liquor store, but once inside, you will soon realize this place is a Château Margaux hidden in a Boones Farm bottle. Bell's selection of wine is surprisingly vast and unique, with many bottles not available anywhere else in the area, and the best part is, the owners are not afraid to open them.

Tastings take place Wednesday evenings and Saturday afternoons. The Saturday afternoon tastings almost have a game show feel to them. Bell selects ten bottles for tasting.

You must taste every bottle in the order specified, no skipping allowed. Many tastings often include high-end treasures at the end, but you have to make it through the questionable bottles before you win the right to try the money wines. The good news: you're allowed to use the slop bucket. The Wednesday tastings are standard affairs during which Bell opens a few favorites for customers to sample, but on the last Wednesday of each month, the store pulls out all the corks. Bell chooses a theme (Champagnes, GSM [a blend of Grenache, Shiraz, and Mourvèdre] wines, etc.) and give customers a chance to try up to 45 bottles, including some of the finest in the shop. And no, you do not have to try them all this time.

Bistrot Lepic & Wine Bar

1736 Wisconsin Ave., NW (at S Street)
(202) 333-0111
www.bistrotlepic.com
Tuesdays, 6 to 8 p.m.

Neighborhood French bistro in Georgetown pours tastes of a few French wines. Join them every Tuesday evening in the upstairs wine bar.

Chevy Chase Wine & Spirits
5544 Connecticut Ave., NW (between Morrison and McKinley Streets)
(202) 363-4000
www.chevychasewine.com
Fridays, 4 to 7 p.m. (beers); Saturdays, 3 to 6 p.m. (beer and wine)

This neighborhood wine and liquor shop has a reputation for being the go-to shop for hard-to-find craft beers in D.C. Chevy Chase shows off its beer selection during tastings every Friday afternoon, and on Saturday afternoons you have your choice of wine or beers.

Circle Wine & Spirits
5501 Connecticut Ave., NW (at Livingstone Street)
(202) 966-0600
www.circlewinelist.com
Saturdays, 1 to 4 p.m., and some Thursday nights

This friendly, neighborhood wine shop uncorks a few bottles every Saturday afternoon. Check out the monthly Thursday evening tasting event. Winemakers and distributors bring in their best bottles for tasting. Typically, one could sample up to twenty-five to thirty wines during these events.

Cleveland Park Wine and Spirits
3423 Connecticut Ave., NW (between Newark and Ordway Streets)
(202) 363-4265
www.clevelandparkwine.com
Wednesdays, 5 to 8 p.m.; Fridays and Saturdays, 4 to 7 p.m.

Neighborhood shop that brings in winemakers and distributors for tastings every Wednesday, Friday, and Saturday evening.

MacArthur Beverages
4877 MacArthur Blvd., NW (at 48th Place)
(202) 338-1433
www.bassins.com
Saturdays, 1 to 4 p.m.

MacArthur Beverages has a vast selection of wines and opens a few bottles during Saturday afternoon tastings.

Magruder's

5626 Connecticut Ave., NW (at Northampton Street)
(202) 244-7800
www.magruders.com
Fridays, 4 to 7 p.m.; Saturdays, 1 to 4 p.m.

A Washington institution, Magruder's is one of the city's last remaining independent grocery stores. The store has an extensive beer, wine, and liquor selection and hosts beer and wine tastings every Friday from 4 to 7 p.m. and Saturdays from 1 to 4 p.m.

Modern Liquors

1200 Ninth St., NW (at M Street)
(202) 289-1414
www.modernliquors.com
Wednesdays, 6 to 8 p.m.

This local liquor shop across the street from the D.C. convention center holds wine and cheese tastings every Wednesday night. On select Friday nights, the shop also holds liquor and beer tastings.

Pearson's

2436 Wisconsin Ave., NW (between Calvert Street and Observatory Road)
(202) 333-6666
www.pearsonswine.com
Saturdays, all day

Picking up a bottle at Pearson's has been a D.C. tradition as far back as Prohibition, when customers needed a prescription in order to get liquor. A few bottles are open for tasting anytime, but on Saturdays, the shop pours twenty to forty bottles during the day.

Schneider's of Capitol Hill

300 Massachusetts Ave., NE (between 3rd and 4th Streets)
(202) 543-9300
www.cellar.com
Saturday afternoons

This small Capitol Hill shop specializes in rare and hard-to-find vintages. Savor a couple of bottles during Saturday tastings.

Vidalia Restaurant

1990 M St., NW (at 20th Street)
(202) 659-1990
www.vidaliadc.com
Mondays to Fridays, 5:30 to 6:30 p.m.

This is one of Washington's best restaurants. Vidalia's sommelier selects two or three of his favorite bottles for customers to taste Monday through Friday from 5:30 to 6:30 p.m. Wines are paired with some artfully prepared treats from the kitchen.

Wide World of Wines

2201 Wisconsin Ave., NW (at W Place)
(202) 333-7500
www.wideworldofwines.com
Saturdays, 1 to 4 p.m.

Wide World of Wines might win the crown for the most elaborate wine tastings in town. Every Saturday afternoon, the shop pours a handful of Rhones or Chiantis. But four or five times a year Wide World conducts a grander tasting that explores a particular region or country. At any one of these tastings, you could be sipping as many as a hundred different wines. These larger tastings take place on Saturdays as well, but the only way to know when is by getting on the shop's e-mail list.

The Wine Specialist
2115 M St., NW (at New Hampshire Avenue)
(202) 833-0707
www.winespecialist.com
http://winespecialist.wordpress.com
Fridays and Saturdays, 5 to 8 p.m.

The good news is that, although the shop is called The Wine Specialist, wine is not all it sells. The better news is that wines are not the only thing they taste. Every Friday and Saturday night from 5 to 8 p.m., wine producers, distributors, or the knowledgeable staff pour wine but often serve selections of beers, liqueurs, or cocktails.

VIRGINIA

Arrowine
4508 Lee Hwy. (between North Woodrow and North Woodstock Streets)
Arlington, VA
(703) 525-0990
www.arrowine.com
Fridays, 5:30 to 7:30 p.m.; Saturdays, 1 to 4 p.m.

Arrowine has a reputation for having a great selection of wine and cheese and a knowledgeable, if somewhat snobby, staff. Get a taste of all three at their tastings every Friday night and Saturday afternoon.

Cork & Fork
7333 Atlas Walk Way (off Gateway Center Drive and Linton Hall Road)
Gainesville, VA
(703) 753-5554
www.corkandforkva.com
Saturdays, 1 to 7 p.m.

Virginia Tastings by the Week

	THURSDAY	FRIDAY	SATURDAY	SUNDAY
Afternoon		The Vineyard Total Wine	Arrowine Cork & Fork Planet Wine Rick's Wine Red, White & Bleu Total Wine The Vineyard	Planet Wine Red, White & Bleu
Evening	Curious Grape	Arrowine Curious Grape Planet Wine Rick's Wine Red, White & Bleu	Curious Grape	

Cork & Fork is a boutique-styled wine and beer store that offers diverse tastings weekly, with anywhere from six to sixteen bottles of wine and four to ten beers being poured on Saturdays.

The Curious Grape

4056 Campbell Ave. (between South Randolph and South Quincy Streets)
Arlington, VA
(703) 671-8700
www.curiousgrape.com
Thursdays, Fridays, and Saturdays, 6 to 8 p.m.

This laid-back wine and chocolate shop hosts winemakers and distributors who uncork a couple of bottles for tasting on Thursday and Friday nights and Saturday afternoons. It also hosts a number of other free tastings and seminars. On most Tuesday nights the shop has more formal, free seminars during which tasters explore different types of wine, as well as food pairings. These are popular events, so reserve a seat. The shop occasionally holds chocolate tastings as well.

Planet Wine Shop

2004 Mt. Vernon Ave. (at E. Howell Avenue)
Alexandria, VA
(703) 549-3444
www.planetwineshop.com
Fridays, 6 to 8 p.m.; Saturdays, 2 to 8 p.m.; Sundays, noon to 5 p.m.

Cozy neighborhood wine shop pops open a few bottles for tastings on the weekends.

Red, White and Bleu

127 South Washington St. (at E Broad Street)
Falls Church, VA
(703) 533-9463
www.redwhiteandbleu.com
Fridays, 5 to 8 p.m.; Saturdays, noon to 8 p.m.; Sundays, 1 to 5 p.m.

This quaint boutique wine and gourmet food shop welcomes customers to try a handful of seasonal wines or beers every Friday night and Saturday and Sunday afternoons. The wines are paired with goodies from their gourmet food section, which may be artisanal cheeses, fine chocolates, or charcuterie.

Rick's Wine and Gourmet

3117 Duke St. (at Sweeley Street)
Alexandria, VA
(703) 823-4600
www.rickswine.com
Fridays, 5 to 8 p.m.; Saturdays, 1 to 5 p.m.; and every night after 5 p.m. (mini tasting)

This friendly wine and gourmet food shop manages to show its personality and taste even though its strip mall location is less than appealing. Every night after 5 p.m. the shop uncorks three bottles for tasting. On Friday nights, winemakers and purveyors bring in a selection of wines for tasting, and on Saturday afternoons, the shop opens several unusual beers for tasting. Cheese and other edibles are available, too.

Total Wine & More

Alexandria, VA, 6240 Little River Turnpike (at Beauregard Street); (703) 941-1133
Chantilly, VA, 13055-C Lee Jackson Memorial Hwy. (Greenbriar Town Center); (703) 817-1177
Fairfax, VA, 9484 Main St. (at Pickett Road); (703) 250-0604
Manassas, VA, 8103 Sudley Rd. (between Lomond Road and Portsmouth Road); (703) 368-2580
McLean, VA, 1451 Chain Bridge Rd. (between Laughlin Avenue and Tennyson Drive); (703) 749-0011
www.totalwine.com
Fridays and Saturdays, noon to 6 p.m.

Total Wine is a chain of magnum-sized wine stores. Each location stocks 8,000 different wines and holds tastings of six to ten wines grouped by region or varietal on Friday and Saturday afternoons. On the days when an official tasting isn't being held, one finds a couple of bottles open for sampling.

The Vineyard

1445 Laughlin Ave. (at Lowell Avenue)
McLean, VA
(703) 288-2970
www.thevineyardva.com
Fridays, 4 to 7 p.m.; Saturdays, 1 to 4 p.m.

Wine and cheese tastings on Friday evenings and Saturday afternoons at this neighborhood wine and gourmet food shop.

HAIR & SPA SERVICES: FREESTYLE

"You'd be surprised how much it costs to look this cheap."
—DOLLY PARTON

Just because your bank account is running low doesn't mean you can't look and feel like a million bucks. Looking good and feeling good can look and feel a whole lot better the less it costs. Anything you need or want done can be had for little to nothing: haircuts, coloring, highlights, facials, makeovers, manicures, and massages. The best places to find free or cheap services are salons with training programs and schools.

HAIR SALONS

Some of the most exclusive (and expensive) salons in the area have training programs for fully licensed hair stylists. These students are always looking for hair. Since these stylists are all licensed and have some experience, getting your hair done is a low-risk proposition. In other words, you can feel reasonably confident you won't end up with an accidental Mohawk. The only catch is that you're sometimes required to spend two to three hours at the salon when you model for a class. Many salons can be picky about whom they use as models; women are used more than men, and longer hair gets you an appointment quicker than shorter hair. The salons listed below offer free cuts and/or color.

De La Inés Salon
5520 Connecticut Ave., Suite 3 (between Morrison and Livingstone Streets)
(202) 362-4280
www.de-la-ines.com

This modern and airy salon, located in the historic Chevy Chase Arcade, has a small, friendly staff that provides high-quality work. Free cuts and color are offered once every other month during its in-house training, usually on a Tuesday night. Call a few days before the salon's training day to make an appointment.

The Grooming Lounge
1745 L St., NW (at 17th Street);
(202) 466-8900
McLean, VA, Tysons Galleria, 1732 U International Dr.;
(703) 288-0355
www.groominglounge.com

The Grooming Lounge is an upscale barbershop that is unlike any barbershop you've ever been to. This men's-only salon and spa, replete with dark wood and classic barber chairs, has all the amenities to make one feel at home, including a wide-screen TV playing ESPN and free root beer, espresso, or even a beer or martini. The lounge needs models for stylist training sessions or to try new products and styles.

Paul Bosserman Salon
3214 N St. (between Wisconsin Avenue and Potomac Street)
(202) 337-0020

The only thing flashy about this small Georgetown salon are the hairstyles. Bosserman is interested in challenging himself and his staff, so if you're open to something new and different, Bosserman or one of his stylists fits you into their busy schedule and works on an artistic and creative new do for you. The salon is usually booked, so these appointments often happen after hours. This is not a formal program; it just happens when Bosserman or his staff are up for it. So make sure to be charming when calling for an appointment.

Saint-Germain by Molécule
439 7th St., NW (between D and E Streets)
(202) 824-0444
www.saintgermainsalon.com

This swanky Penn Quarter salon uses models for cuts and colors by assistants on a regular basis but not all the time. Saint-Germain is the only official L'Oréal Professional Haircolor Center in the area, so classes and training sessions will involve color.

Salon Cielo
1741 Connecticut Ave. (between R and S Streets)
(202) 518-9620
www.saloncielo.com

The Catch You must be willing to let them style your hair however they want to.

This stylish Aveda Concept salon uses hair-adventurous models for its Wednesday evening class, which works on new styles and techniques. Call a week or two in advance to set up an appointment, which is free, minus the cost of the materials for color (usually around $20). A free blow-drying session is offered on the last Friday night of the month, complete with wine and cheese. Reservations required.

Sassoon Salon
McLean, VA, Tysons Galleria, 1855G International Dr. (At Chain Bridge Road)
(703) 448-9884
(703) 761-9666 (assistant appointment line)
www.sassoon.com

The Catch You must be willing to let them do whatever they want to your hair.

Several times a year, Vidal Sassoon's creative director flies in from the salon's headquarters in London to D.C. to share his new creations with the local team of stylists and colorists. Hair models are needed and must be willing to let the stylists do anything to their hair. To become a house model, meet with a staff member at the salon, who will take your picture. Not all prospective models are picked; it depends on the kind of hair they are looking for at the time. During the year, house models are used for other projects. If you are more interested in walking down Main Street than a runway, you can book low-priced cuts and colors with an assistant.

Ted Gibson Salon & Hela Spa @ The Collection
Chevy Chase, MD, 5481 Wisconsin Ave., Level 2 (between Willard and South Park Avenue)
(301) 951-4445
www.tedgibsonsalon.com

This is a D.C. offshoot of the plush New York salon, where Ted Gibson is hairstylist to the stars and counts Angelina Jolie, Renee Zellweger, Keira Knightley, Anne Hathaway, and Oprah as his clients. Gibson charges upwards of $900 for a snip, but every Wednesday night, the salon's assistants need heads to practice new styles and techniques.

Tenley Studio by PR at Partners
4000 Wisconsin Ave., NW (between Upton and Rodman Streets)
(202) 966-7780
tenleystudio@gmail.com
www.tenleystudio.com
www.pratpartners.com

Get a new look from Tenley Studio by PR at Partners every other Sunday and Monday. A string of fun, stylish, and hip salons that pride themselves on transforming your look, PR at Partners offers free cuts and colors on Mondays when artistic director Sean Stredwick takes a break from working with top models in Miami to coach the salon's stylists. He challenges and tweaks their techniques to get you looking like one of his Miami models. Only stylists with three years' experience are allowed to work on your hair. Appointments run from 10 a.m. to 4 p.m., so set aside two hours of salon time.

LOW PRICED/**HIGH** STYLE

One80 Salon
1275 K St., NW (between 12th and 13th Streets)
(202) 842-9113
www.one80salon.com

The Catch $25 for appointments with assistants.

This warm, modern salon, considered one of Washington's best by local critics, caters to the professional set. Regular cuts are $90, but during training sessions, the salon only charges $25 to $50 for appointments.

Salon Jean-Paul
4820 Yuma St., NW (between 48th and 49th Streets)
(202) 966-4600

Salon Jean-Paul has been cutting the hair of D.C.'s elite for more than thirty-five years but was sold in early 2009, and as of press time the new owners are implementing a training program. They expect to charge about half the regular price ($75 and up) for cuts with the assistants.

Urban Style Lab
1314 Connecticut Ave. (between N Street and Massachusetts Avenue)
(202) 223-2066
www.lab-dc.com

The Catch $10 for appointments with assistants.

Urban Style Lab's mission is to be "Washington's most fashion-forward hair salon" so budding hipsters and fashionistas flock to this funky salon. During training sessions, Urban Style Lab only charges $10 for a cut (normally $75).

BEAUTY & ESTHETICS SCHOOLS

These schools train students for the state licensing exam, so the amount of experience and skill fluctuates greatly from student to student. You take a chance with these stylists, so they often make you sign a release before you get your haircut. The students are supervised, but the level of supervision varies from place to place. A number of these schools also prepare students to become estheticians and offer student clinics for facials and skin care. There are quite a few beauty schools in the area, from large conglomerates such as Aveda, Paul Mitchell, and Graham Webb to smaller facilities. Aveda and the like are nationally accredited, have modern salonlike facilities, and turn out students heading to high-end salons. The prices for services at these schools are pretty steep once you get past the basic cut and blow-dry. The smaller facilities aren't necessarily accredited, have somewhat rundown facilities, and are more likely to turn out stylists for neighborhood beauty parlors and budget-minded salons. The prices at these schools are lower, but the quality may be as well.

Name-Brand Schools

Aveda Institute Washington, D.C.
713 7th St., NW (at Gallery Place)
(800) 884-3588 or (202) 824-1624
www.avedainstitutedc.com

Cut and simple style: $18 to $25, color: $25 to $80, facials: $45.

Graham Webb Academy
1621 North Kent St., Suite 1617 LL (between Lynn Street and Wilson Boulevard)
Arlington, VA
(703) 243-9322 ext. 101
www.grahamwebbacademyonline.com

Haircuts: $10 men, $18 women; color: $40 and up; manicures: $12; facials: $40; waxing: $8 to $50.

Paul Mitchell Hair Expressions Academy
12450 Parklawn Dr. (at Twinbrook Parkway)
Rockville, MD
(301) 984-0566
www.hairex.com

Haircuts: $10 to $13, manicures: $7 to $11, color: $30 and up.

Paul Mitchell the School—Virginia
8090-L Tysons Corner Center (at Leesburg Pike)
McLean, VA
(703) 288-0008
www.pmtsvirginia.com

Haircuts: $12 to $17, color: $37 and up. Each haircut includes a five-minute stress-relieving scalp treatment.

Rugs, a Blender and a Makeover

Whenever you need professional beauty assistance, stop by any makeup counter at finer department stores and have a professional makeup artist do the work for you. The counters at **Macy's** (1201 G. St., NW, at 12th Street; 202-628-6661), **Lord & Taylor** (5255 Western Ave. at Cortland Road, 202-362-9600), **Saks Fifth Avenue** (5555 Wisconsin Ave., Chevy Chase, MD, 301-657-9000), and **Neiman Marcus at Mezze Gallery** (5300 Wisconsin Ave., NW, at Western Avenue) all offer free makeovers using their pricey products. You can also stop by for a touch-up or more at cosmetic stores such as **M.A.C.** (3067 M St., NW, at 31st Street, 202-944-9771), **Blue Mercury** (1619 Connecticut Ave., NW, between Q and R Streets, 202-462-1300) or **Sephora** (1100 South Hayes St. at South 15th Street, Arlington, VA, 703-415-4501).

Yvonne de Vilar
305 Maple Ave West (between Pleasant and Lewis Streets)
Vienna, VA
(703) 281-2070
www.scientificskincare.com

Facials: $42, body treatments and tanning: $30 to $40, waxing: $6 to $45.

Generic

American Beauty Academy
Wheaton Campus
11006 Viers Mill Rd. (at Georgia Avenue)
Wheaton, MD
(301) 949-3000
www.americanbeautyacademy.org

Haircuts: $8, manicures: $7, pedicures: $15, braids: $20 to $45.

Esthetic Institute
2112 B Gallows Rd. (between Wolftrap Road and Merry Oaks Lane)
Vienna, VA
(703) 288-4228
www.esthetic-institute.com

Facials: $30, massages: $35. Check the Web site for coupons for free waxing.

Hair Academy
8435 Annapolis Rd. (between 85th Avenue and Riverdale Road)
New Carrollton, MD
(301) 459-2509
www.hairacademymd.com

Haircuts for women only: $10 to $12, manicures: $7, pedicures: $12.

Heritage Institute
8255 Shoppers Sq. (off Centerville Road)
Manassas, VA
(703) 334-2517
www.heritage-education.com

Heritage is a national technical college with stylist and massage therapy programs. Shampoo and cut: $10, massages: $25.

Montgomery Beauty School
8736 Arliss St. (between Flower Avenue and Piney Branch Road)
Silver Spring, MD
(301) 588-3570
www.montgomerybeautyschool.com

Haircuts: $9, manicures: $8.

MASSAGE SCHOOL STUDENT CLINICS

Yes, it is possible to get a free massage. At two massage school clinics, the therapists manipulate your muscles without asking for a handout. Other student clinics are not free, but you can get a a relaxing massage for less than half of what you'd pay at a spa or gym in the area. Of course, you shouldn't expect spa amenities at these clinics; bring your own cucumber water and herbal eye pillow. Students have spent the last 500 hours or so practicing on each other and are ready to work on real clients. The massages you receive at the clinic will be professional in style, but the quality of the therapist's work runs the gamut from ahhhh-mazing to can-you-please-use-a-little-more-pressure. If you prefer a more intense massage, a number of graduates and faculty do offer their services, for a price. Most clinics only service clients on limited days and hours and do require appointments.

Free Student Clinics

Centura College
6295 Edsall Rd., Suite 250 (exit 2 of US 395)
Alexandria, VA
(703) 778-4444
www.centuracollege.edu

Centura College is a large technical school with programs in massage therapy. Students complete more than 700 hours in massage training before they practice on anyone other than fellow students. The college runs a small student clinic that offers free massages to the public Monday to Thursday from 10 a.m. to noon. Villa Centura, the school's Tuscan-themed "spa," is one of the rare student clinics at which you have a private treatment room. Massages aren't offered every week, so call ahead to make an appointment.

Everest College
1430 Springhill Rd., Suite 200 (at International Drive)
McLean, VA
(703) 288-3131
www.everest.edu

The atmosphere at Everest College isn't quite as luxurious as Centura (massages are conducted in a large room with curtained-off private areas), but it's rare for a customer to wait long to get in for a free massage. Choose from a chair massage or a thirty-minute or one-hour regular massage. The clinic runs every Wednesday from 1 to 7 p.m.

Student Clinics with a Fee

AKS Massage School
Springwood Professional Center
462 Herndon Parkway, Suite 104 (off Spring Street)
Herndon, VA
(703) 464-9352
www.aksmassageschool.com

This small massage school offers student clinics at various times throughout the year. Student massages are $40 for an hour. Appointments with staff and graduates start at $45.

Heritage Institute
8255 Shoppers Sq. (off Centerville Road)
Manassas, VA
(703) 334-2517
www.heritage-education.com

Heritage is a technical college with locations across the country. The Manassas location has a limited number of appointments available Monday to Thursday at 9 a.m., 1:30 p.m., and 6 p.m. during the year. The clinic is popular, so appointments fill up quickly. Be persistent. Sessions are $25 for a one-hour massage.

National Massage Therapy Institute
803 W Broad St. (between Spring and Oak Streets)
Falls Church, VA
(800) 509-5058
www.studymassage.com

The National Massage Therapy Institute is part of a chain of massage schools with locations throughout the country. The facilities are clean and modern, and appointments are available every Monday, Tuesday, and Wednesday from 9 a.m. to 8 p.m. $35 for a one-hour massage.

Northern Virginia School of Therapeutic Massage
200 Little Falls St., Suite 303 (at Park Avenue)
Falls Church, VA
(703) 888-9782
www.nvschoolofmassage.com

The Northern Virginia School of Therapeutic Massage only admits fifty students at a time. Student massages are available every Wednesday at 12:15 p.m., 1:30 p.m., 5:30 p.m., and 6:45 p.m., as well as on Saturday at 11 a.m. and noon. Appointments are easy to come by; call a few days to a week in advance. $35 for a one-hour massage.

Potomac Massage Training Institute
5028 Wisconsin Ave., NW, Suite LL (between Garrison and Fessenden Streets)
(202) 686-7046
www.pmti.org

The Potomac Massage Training Institute is considered to be one of the leading massage schools in the country. Student clinic appointments take place in a private room and are available every week on Tuesday afternoons and evenings, Wednesday evenings, Thursday afternoons, and Friday and Saturday mornings. You can also make appointments with recent graduates of the program, as well as faculty members and established professionals. Student clinic appointments are $37, graduate clinic appointments are $55, and professional appointments are $80 for one-hour massages.

Thai Institute of Healing Arts

1211 North Glebe Rd. (between Washington Boulevard and 13th Street)
Arlington, VA
(571) 344-3333
www.thai-institute.com

The Thai Insitute of Healing Arts specializes in traditional Thai massage, which is not your standard rubdown. Clients are fully clothed, and no oil is used, but you're still pulled, stretched, and pushed into unexpected positions. Student massages are $45 for an hour. Faculty and professional appointments are $65. Appointments are available on various days every month.

CHILDREN'S EVENTS AND ACTIVITIES:
FREE TO BE YOU AND ME

*"We've begun to long for the pitter-patter
of little feet — so we bought a dog.
Well, it's cheaper, and you get more feet."*
—RITA RUDNER

Washington, D.C., is an amazing place for kids and not just for those who can afford to attend Sidwell Friends School. Besides the Air and Space Museum, the memorials and monuments, the Capitol and the White House, children of all ages enjoy the parks and public spaces. story times, classes, movies, and performances that don't cost their parents too much.

DESTINATION PLAYGROUNDS

Clemyjontri Park
6317 Georgetown Pike (between Dolly Madison Boulevard and Chain Bridge Road)
McLean, VA
(703) 388-2807
www.fairfaxcounty.gov/parks/clemyjontri

This unique park has more than its fair share of fun swings, slides, and monkey bars, but the truly wonderful thing is "children of all abilities can play side-by-side" here. The two-acre, themed playground is designed to be fully accessible. Each of the four separate play areas has special equipment to encourage children with and without disabilities to enjoy playing together. The play areas encircle a classic carousel ($1.50 a ride), which is also fully accessible.

Turtle Park
45th Street, NW, & Van Ness Street
(202) 282-2198
www.turtlepark.org

Turtle Park is ranked as one of the best parks in Washington and with good reason. It has a large enclosed playground with plenty of equipment for children of all ages, a popular sprayground where kids can cool off in the summer, and, its most distinctive feature, a huge sandbox with a large stone turtle and plenty of digging equipment. During the winter the park hosts story time and crafts every afternoon in the recreation center and stories on Saturday morning.

Wheaton Regional Park Adventure Playground
2000 Shorefield Rd. (near Georgia Avenue)
Wheaton, MD
(301) 680-3803
www.montgomeryparks.org

Your children's eyes may pop out of their heads when they get a look at this playground. To say that the playground has swings, slides, and never-ending climbing structures just doesn't do it justice. It's the size of the playground and the variety of equipment that's astonishing. Home to Brookside Gardens and Nature Center, Wheaton Regional Park also boasts its own turn-of-the-century carousel and miniature train that you can ride ($1.75 a ride). Brookside is always free and offers many activities for families as well.

STORY TIMES

Barnes & Noble
Washington, D.C.
Downtown D.C., 555 12th St., NW (at E Street); (202) 347-0176; Tuesday mornings
Georgetown, 3040 M St., NW (at Thomas Jefferson Street); (202) 965-9880; Friday and Wednesday mornings

Maryland
Bethesda, 4801 Bethesda Ave. (at Woodmont Avenue); (301) 986-1761; Saturday mornings
Rockville Pike, Montrose Crossing, 12089 Rockville Pike (at Montrose Road); (301) 881-0237; Friday nights and Saturday mornings

Virginia
Arlington, 2800 Clarendon Blvd. (at North Edgewood Street); (703) 248-8244; Wednesday and Saturday mornings
Tysons Corner Mall, 7851 L. Tysons Corner Center (at Leesburg Pike); (703) 506-2937; Wednesday mornings
Falls Church, 6260 Seven Corners Center (on Arlington Boulevard); (703) 536-0774; Tuesday mornings
www.barnesandnoble.com

Barnes & Noble bookstores host a plethora of free readings and events for kids and adults. The local stores hold story times every week during which B & N staff, authors, costumed characters, and other guests gather children around to hear a book, sing songs, and make crafts. All story-time events are geared for children six and under.

Brookside Gardens
1800 Glenallan Ave. (just off Randolph Road)
Wheaton, MD
(301) 962-1400
www.brooksidegardens.org

Montgomery County's lovely Brookside Gardens holds a story time every Saturday morning for three- to six-year-olds with seasonal stories about nature. Every week the stories are followed by a crafts project. Brookside also offers many other regular classes and activities, but they do charge a small fee for those.

Jabberu
Bethesda, MD, 4926 Del Ray Ave. (between Old Georgetown Road and Norfolk Avenue)
Gaithersburg, MD, 316 Main St. (in The Kentlands)
(301) 951-1101
www.jabberu.com

Jabberu is a foreign language school for children from twelve months to ten years old. Classes aren't free, but on Tuesday mornings at 11:35 a.m. (Bethesda) and 11:15 a.m. (Gaithersburg), everyone is welcome to attend the French and English story time and sing-along. The school also organizes a Bastille Day celebration and other free global cultural events throughout the year.

Kinder Haus Toys
1220 North Fillmore St. (at Clarenden Boulevard)
Arlington, VA
www.kinderhaus.com

The Catch Your child will beg you to buy a toy or two from the store.

Kinder Haus is a family-run toy and bookstore that's brimming with goodies any child would enjoy. Story time happens every Monday and Friday morning. Be careful, however, as you might be tempted to buy something from the store's unique selection, and the prices aren't necessarily cheap.

National Air and Space Museum—National Mall

Independence Avenue at 6th Street, SW
(202) 633-1000
www.nasm.si.edu

Of course the National Air and Space Museum is a wonderland for kids anytime, but on Friday and Saturday mornings they ignite children's imaginations with "Flights of Fancy," a story-time and crafts series for pre-schoolers to 2nd graders. The staff and guest readers weave stories about astronauts, hot-air balloon flights, trips to outer space, stars and planets, and winged creatures.

National Building Museum

401 F St., NW (between 4th and 5th Streets)
(202) 272-2448
www.nbm.org

Take your toddler to the Building Museum the first Tuesday morning of the month for the Book of the Month club, during which the staff and guest readers share a well-known book about building, construction, or cities.

National Gallery of Art

4th and Constitution Avenue, NW (between 3rd and 9th Streets)
(202) 737-4215
www.nga.gov

Take a trip around the art world during the "Summer Stories Series" at the National Gallery of Art. Every summer the gallery uses its vast collection as a starting point for stories and activities that explore a country's artwork. The series runs on Sundays, Mondays, and Tuesdays during July and August with several sessions each day. Space is limited to the first seventy children to sign up for each session, but no advanced reservations are accepted; to participate, sign up in the lobby the morning of the event. It pays to make a habit of it, as the museum dispenses prizes to kids that take part in three or more sessions.

National Museum of African Art
950 Independence Ave., SW (between 7th and 14th Streets)
(202) 633-4600
http://africa.si.edu

"Let's Read About Africa" introduces young readers to Africa through stories and craft projects. Readings take place on the first Saturday of the month and are meant for five- to ten-year-olds. The National Museum of African Art also hosts workshops, films, and performances for young people.

Check It Out!

Instead of your local librarian shushing you, she wants you and your children to make a racket. Story time at the library can be a lively affair at just about any branch in D.C., Maryland, and Virginia. An event occurs almost any day of the week, and some branches have as many as two or three different sessions a day. Some are geared toward babies, others toward toddlers and school-age children. These get-togethers almost always include a few songs, stories, nursery rhymes, and a big crate full of toys for the kids to tussle over.

Washington, D.C.: www.dclibrary.org

Arlington, VA: www.arlingtonva.us/Departments/Libraries/LibrariesMain.aspx#

Alexandria, VA: www.alexandria.lib.va.us

Montgomery County, MD: www.montgomerycountymd.gov/Library

Prince George's County: www.prge.lib.md.us

National Museum of the American Indian

Fourth Street & Independence Avenue, SW
(202) 633-1000
www.nmai.si.edu

After attending one of the two regularly scheduled story times at the National Museum of the American Indian, you'll be able to answer "Yes" to this question: "Hok-noth-da?" The Shawnee phrase, which means "Did you hear?" is the name of the story times for grade-schoolers, held on the morning of the first and third Wednesday of the month. Younger children enjoy the twice-daily story times.

Politics and Prose Bookstore

5015 Connecticut Ave., NW
(202) 364-1919
www.politics-prose.com

Bring your babies and toddlers to the store for a song-filled, interactive story time every Monday morning. The Politics and Prose Bookstore hosts other children's events, including a poetry workshop for children ten and up the last Sunday of the month.

Smithsonian American Art Museum

8th and F Streets, NW
(202) 633-1000
www.americanart.si.edu

The Smithsonian American Art Museum hosts family days on the second Saturday of the month. Kids and parents will enjoy storytelling, arts and crafts activities and musical performances.

Turtle Park

45th & Van Ness, NW
(202) 282-2198
www.turtlepark.org

During the winter months, the fun moves indoors at this lively community park. From January through March, children up to six years old are welcome to attend Turtle Time, an afternoon of arts and crafts projects that take place every Monday through Friday. On Saturday mornings, it's story time with Larry "The Reader Dude."

FAMILY FILMS

AMC Summer Camp

AMC Hoffman Center 22
206 Swamp Fox Rd. (between Mandville Lane and Eisenhower Avenue)
Alexandria, VA
(888) 262-4386
(703) 236-1083
www.amctheaters.com/smc

The Catch Admission is $1, but it goes to charity.

Instead of dropping $10 to see a movie at this AMC Theater, just donate $1 to its partner charity and you're in any Wednesday morning in June and July. The theater shows recent animated and live-action hits.

Historical Society of Washington
801 K St., NW (at Mount Vernon Square)
(202) 383-1850
www.historydc.org

The Historical Society of Washington hosts monthly screenings of crowd-pleasing family films such as *E.T.* and *Miracle on 34th Street*.

Montgomery County Public Libraries
www.montgomerycountymd.gov/Library

Many of the Montgomery County Public Library branches show feature films and shorter videos for children as young as two years old.

National Gallery of Art
4th and Constitution Avenue, NW (between 3rd and 9th Streets)
(202) 737-4215
www.nga.gov

You won't see recent blockbusters at the National Gallery of Art. But the gallery's film program screens the world's finest art films for young audiences. Often these are the only area showings of these movies fresh from the film festival circuit. Screenings take place one weekend every month, and entrance is on a first-come, first-served basis.

Phoenix Theaters

Union Station 9 Theaters, 50 Massachusetts Ave. (between 1st and F Streets); (202) 842-4455
Worldgate 9 Theatres, 13025 Worldgate Dr. (at Centerville Road); Herndon, VA; (703) 318-9290
www.phoenixtheatres.com

The Phoenix Movie Theaters show two recent crowd pleasers (one G- and one PG-rated film) every Tuesday and Wednesday morning in July and August. If you want a snack during the movie, the kiddie combo of popcorn, candy, and soda is only $5.

Regal Theaters

www.regmovies.com (click on Now Showing)

Maryland
Majestic Stadium 20, 900 Ellsworth Dr. (at Fenton Street), Silver Spring; (301) 565-8884

Virginia
Fairfax Towne Center 10, 4110 West Ox Rd. (between Monument Drive and Legato Road), Fairfax; (703) 591-4994
Fox Stadium 16, 22875 Brambleton Plaza (Ryan Road and Northstar Boulevard), Ashburn; (703) 957-1027
Kingstowne Stadium 16, 5910 Kingstowne Towne Center (between Kingstowne Boulevard and Kingstowne Village Parkway), Alexandria; (703) 719-0784
Manassas Stadium 14, 11380 Bulloch Dr. (Parkridge Center), Manassas; (703) 366-2842
Potomac Yard Stadium 16, 3575 Jefferson Davis Hwy. (at E Reed Avenue), Alexandria; (703) 739-4054

National chain Regal Cinemas shows recent kid-friendly movies at 10 a.m. on Tuesdays and Wednesdays from June to August. Tickets are dispensed at the box office.

Shirlington Branch Library

4200 Campbell Ave. (in Shirlington Village)
Arlington, VA
(703) 228-6545
http://shirlingtonlibrary.wordpress.com

Bring the kids to the Shirlington Branch Library for G-rated family films on the first and third of the month. It also shows a slew of other films for children and adults every month.

ARTS, CRAFTS, & PERFORMANCES

Chinatown Cultural Community Center
616 H St., NW (between 6th and 7th Streets)
(202) 628-1688
www.ccccdc.org
www.wongpeople.com

Give your kids their recommended daily allowance of kicks and "Hiii-Yaaas!" without having to spending all your money. The Wong People is a volunteer organization that teaches kids and adults a non-commercial form of kung fu. You won't be pressured to buy special outfits or equipment or be forced to advance through many different levels. Classes focus more on the culture of the martial art and less on the combat. Kids' classes are scheduled to coordinate with free adult tai chi or kung fu classes.

Corcoran ArtReach at THEARC
1901 Mississippi Ave., SE (at 19th Street)
(202) 889-5088
www.thearcdc.org

If you've always thought your child's artwork deserved to hang in a better place than on your refrigerator, the Corcoran Gallery can help. For more than fifteen years, the gallery's art educators have offered free art classes to Washington, D.C., children and given them a chance to show their work in the museum. ArtReach classes take place on weekday afternoons at THEARC and run for a semester at a time. Students take field trips to explore the art of the Corcoran and create their own artwork inspired by their experiences. Registration is required, but no prior art experience is necessary.

Hirshhorn Museum and Sculpture Garden
Independence Avenue and Seventh Street SW
(202) 633-1000
www.hirshhorn.si.edu

The Hirshhorn, the Smithsonian's home for modern and contemporary art, helps young artists create contemporary art as they work with visiting artists. Children create their own pieces inspired by their imagination and the museum's exhibitions. Separate workshops exist for six- to nine-year-olds, ten- to thirteen-year-olds and teenagers. Registration is required.

ImaginAsia
Freer/Sacker Galleries
1150 Jefferson Dr., SW (at 12th Street)
(202) 633-1000
www.asia.si.edu

Hands-on Asian crafts and activities for children aged eight to fourteen. Learn the history and craft behind Japanese anime and Korean paper bowls and kites, as well as other Asian art while creating your own. Workshops change every month but are held Saturdays and Sundays on a drop-in basis.

Lebanese Taverna
Arlington, VA, 5900 Washington Blvd. (at McKinley Road); (703) 241-8681
Bethesda, MD, 7141 Arlington Rd. (at Elm Street); (301) 951-8681
www.lebanesetaverna.com

The Arlington and Bethesda locations of this popular Middle Eastern restaurant are not just a great place to get a delicious fattoush salad and falafel. Bring the kids on Tuesday mornings in Bethesda or Wednesday mornings in Arlington for puppet shows, performances, and stories from a rotating corps of local entertainers, including Banjo Man, Groovy Nate, and Oh Susannah! Hang around after the show for lunch and the kids eat free, as long as Mom or Dad buys lunch as well.

Millennium Stage
The Kennedy Center
2700 F St., NW (at 25th Street)
(202) 467-4600
www.kennedy-center.org/programs/millennium

Every day at 6 p.m. the Kennedy Center presents a free performance on the Millennium Stage. While the performances are not exclusively for children, just about everything the center presents can be enjoyed by a young audience. Daily performances run the gamut from classical music, jazz, and popular music to theater, dance, and circus performances. Check out the Instrument Petting Zoo, a unique event during which children get an up-close experience with the instruments of the orchestra. The Petting Zoo takes place an hour before each National Symphony Orchestra family concert. The concerts aren't free, but the Petting Zoo is.

National Building Museum
401 F St., NW (between 4th and 5th Streets)
(202) 272-2448
www.nbm.org

In a building that is an architectural wonder, children can wonder, experiment, and learn the basic concepts of building and construction in the Building Zone. Younger kids enjoy playing with the trucks and bulldozers, donning hard hats, and putting their construction skills to the test with Legos and other building blocks. On weekends, children over five participate in construction workshops to learn about arches, trusses, and bridges. Registration is required for the weekend classes.

National Children's Museum Launch Zone
112 Waterfront St. (off National Harbor Boulevard)
National Harbor, MD
(301) 686-0225
www.ccm.org

When the expansive National Children's Museum opens in 2013, it will be a wonderland of activities, exhibits, and workshops for children of all ages, but until then you can get a hint of what's to come at the Launch Zone. The Launch Zone has hands-on exhibits about the building of the new state-of-the-art museum designed by world-renowned architect Cesar Pelli. Performances and activities are planned at the Launch Zone. Open daily, 10 a.m. to 5 p.m. except Sundays, when it opens at 11 a.m.

National Gallery of Art
4th and Constitution Avenue, NW (between 3rd and 9th Streets)
(202) 737-4215
www.nga.gov

Young artists' imaginations are put to work at hands-on workshops with artists and museum educators. Classes tour one of the gallery's exhibitions and create works of art inspired by the art on the walls. Registration is required.

National Portrait Gallery
8th and F Streets, NW
(202) 633-8300
(202) 633-8501 (class registration)
www.npg.si.edu

About once a month at the National Portrait Gallery, children aged ten to fourteen take part in a two-hour class exploring the work of one artist and make their own pieces of art based on it. Space is limited, so call to register.

Sports in the City

David Beckham had to start somewhere, and the next Beckham, Derek Jeter, or Michael Phelps can start at a Washington, D.C., recreation center. Sixty-two recreation and community centers are spread across the city, and a wealth of activities for young and old are offered. Everything from Tiny Tots Soccer leagues to line dancing classes for seniors. Many of the classes are free for youths aged three to six years, including soccer, Pee Wee Flag Football, Tee Ball, and swimming classes. Other free classes for older children include belly dancing and cooking. Still, other classes and leagues aren't free but are relatively inexpensive. For more information, log on to the D.C. **Department of Recreation's Web site** at **www.dpr.dc.gov/dpr.**

The National Theatre

1321 Pennsylvania Ave. (between 13th and 14th Streets)
(202) 783-3372
www.nationaltheatre.org

The National Theatre hosts a series of free family performances on most Saturday mornings from September to May. The entertainers vary but have included circus performers, puppet shows, musicals and plays, magicians, ventriloquists, vaudeville performers, costume characters, and even a dancing dog or two. Shows start at 9:30 a.m. and 11 a.m., and tickets are given out thirty minutes before each show.

Reston Museum

1639 Washington Plaza (Lake Anne Village Center)
Reston, VA
(703) 709-7700
www.restonmuseum.org

Local artist Pat McIntyre teaches a very popular art workshop at the Reston Museum every Saturday morning from 10 a.m. to noon.

The Textile Museum

2320 S St., NW (between 23rd and 24th Streets)
(202) 667-0441
www.textilemuseum.org

The Textile Museum rolls out the red carpet for families the afternoon of the first Saturday of the month. The Free First Saturday activities include storytelling and crafts such as quilting or rug making.

United States Botanic Gardens

100 Maryland Ave., SW (at 3rd Street)
(202) 225-8333
www.usbg.gov

Children three to five enjoy "Sprouts," a plant-based playtime that includes storytelling crafts and walks around the garden, on Wednesday mornings monthly. Registration is required.

Wolf Trap

1551 Trap Rd. (off SR 267, Dulles Toll Road)
Vienna, VA
(703) 255-1824
www.nps.gov/wotr

From late June to early August the performers at the Children's Theatre-in-the-Woods at Wolf Trap National Park lead workshops for children five and up. Held on Tuesday, Thursday, and Saturday mornings, kids learn dance, theater games, puppetry, or singing. Reservations are required.

FUN WITH SCIENCE & HISTORY

Goddard Space Flight Center's Visitor Center

ICESat Road and Greenbelt Road (SR 193)
(301) 286-3978
www.nasa.gov/centers/goddard/visitor

The people that inspire the sentence, "I want to be an astronaut when I grow up" want to inspire your kids to be scientists and engineers as well. The Sunday Experiment takes place on the third Sunday of the month at the Goddard Space Flight Center and gives children and adults the chance to perform amazing hands-on activities, such as building rockets and hovercrafts and designing your own planets and stars, while working alongside NASA scientists and engineers. If you can't get enough, be sure to visit Goddard on the first Sunday of the month when they host public model-rocket launches.

National Museum of American History

14th Street and Constitution Avenue, NW
(202) 633-1000
www.americanhistory.si.edu

The telephone, television, and computer were all born out of someone's imagination. Spark!Lab at the National Museum of American History wants your child to be the next great inventor. The lab allows visitors the chance

Feed Me!

Taking the family out to dinner can certainly put a dent in your wallet. The tab for a family of four at a basic restaurant can easily run upwards of $60, and that's if you stay away from the Bloomin' Onion and Nachos Grande. But if you time it right, a handful of area restaurants can trim your check. These eateries have special nights when they let the kids eat free. Of course, examine the fine print before dining at these establishments. Usually, kids can only order from a limited children's menu, and adults must order from the regular menu.

Argonaut Tavern

1433 H St. (at Maryland Avenue)
(202) 397-1416
http://argonautdc.com
Wednesday nights

Austin Grill Alexandria

801 King St. (at N Columbus Street), Alexandria, VA
(703) 684-8969
www.austingrill.com
Tuesday nights

Austin Grill Bethesda

7278 Woodmont Ave. (at Bethesda Avenue), Bethesda, MD
(301) 656-1366
www.austingrill.com
Tuesday nights

Hard Times Cafe Bethesda

4920 Delray Ave. (off Old Georgetown Road), Bethesda, MD
(301) 951-3300
www.hardtimes.com
Tuesday nights

Hard Times Cafe Rockville

1117 Nelson St. (near Azalea Drive), Rockville, MD
(301) 294-9720
www.hardtimes.com
Thursday nights

Kemble Park Tavern
5125 MacArthur Blvd., NW (at Dana Place)
(202) 966-5125
www.kembleparktavern.com
Sunday nights from 5 to 7 p.m.

Lebanese Taverna Arlington
5900 Washington Blvd. (at McKinley Road), Arlington, VA
(703) 241-8681
www.lebanesetaverna.com
Wednesday afternoons

Lebanese Taverna Bethesda
7141 Arlington Rd. (at Elm Street), Bethesda, MD
(301) 951-8681
www.lebanesetaverna.com
Tuesday afternoons

Mr. Henry's Capitol Hill
601 Pennsylvania Ave. SE (at 6th Street)
(202) 546-8412
www.mrhenrysrestaurant.com
Tuesdays from 5:30 to 9 p.m.

Old Glory Bar-B-Que
3139 M St. NW (off Wisconsin Avenue)
(202) 337-3406
www.oldglorybbq.com
Sunday and Monday nights from 4 to 9 p.m.

Red Hot & Blue
4150 Chain Bridge Rd. (at Judicial Drive); Fairfax, VA
(703) 218-6989
Monday nights

Check for up-to-date listings of "Kids Eat Free" specials at these sites:
www.mykidseatfree.info: Lists Northern Virginia restaurants as well as other bargains in the area.
www.kidseat4free.com: Lists national chain restaurants with "Kids Eat Free" deals.

to work with the tools you'd need to invent something in an effort to spark your imagination. The many activities are geared to take you through every step of inventing a new product—think it, explore it, sketch it, create it, try it, tweak it, and sell it. Most activities are for children over six, but toddlers aren't left out. The lab runs from 10 a.m. to 4 p.m. daily, and no reservation is required.

National Museum of Health and Medicine
Walter Reed Army Medical Center
6900 Georgia Ave., NW (at Elder Street), Building 54
(202) 782-2200
www.nmhm.washingtondc.museum

Take your budding CSI to the National Museum of Health and Medicine for some practical experience analyzing DNA, fingerprinting, and other fun forensic activities. The workshops take place every other Saturday afternoon.

National Wildlife Visitor Center
North Track, off SR 198 (east of the Baltimore/Washington Parkway);
(301) 497-5887
Laurel, MD, South Track, 10901 Scarlet Tanager Loop (off Power Mill Road at Baltimore/Washington Parkway); (301) 497-5580
www.fws.gov/northeast/patuxent

Less than thirty minutes from downtown D.C. lies a 12,000-acre wildlife refuge operated by the U.S. Fish and Wildlife Service called the National Wildlife Visitor Center. The public has access to two sections of this vast swath of land and water: The North Track is open to the public for hunting and fishing but also has camps, classes, hikes, and programs for kids age three and up. Get your hands on frogs, search the woods for owls, or create beautiful works of art with wildflowers. Classes for the youngest nature lover are full of songs, stories, and crafts, and the budding teenage environmentalist can wander the woods with a staff naturalist to learn about the wildlife at the refuge. If you're age five to thirteen, don't miss the two- or three-day nature-intensive mini-camps during the summer. Registration is required for most programs and all mini-camps.

The South Track is home to the Visitor Center. Part zoo, part museum, part laboratory, the center is filled with interactive exhibits and fun ways to learn about wildlife, endangered species, and the work of wildlife researchers. Kids can take part in many classes and programs at the center as well.

Thirty-minute guided tram tours of the refuge are available spring to fall ($3 for adults, $2 for seniors, $1 for children under 12). Or if you'd rather explore the refuge on your own, the friendly staff will suggest several hiking trails. Open 9 a.m. to 4:30 p.m. every day except federal holidays.

Oxon Hill Farm

6411 Oxon Hill Rd. (just off exit 3A of I-95)
Oxon Hill, MD
www.nps.gov/archive/nace/oxhi

After reading *The Big Red Barn* to your children a thousand times, why not give them a taste of the real thing? Oxon Hill is a 512-acre working farm run by the National Park Service that operates as any farm would have in the early 20th century. Visitors can milk the cows, work with chickens, or take a wagon trip around the farm. Kids enjoy petting the goats, horses, rabbits, and other four-legged residents. Some reservations are required.

Rock Creek Nature Center and Planetarium

5200 Glover Rd., NW
(202) 895-6070
www.nps.gov/rocr

Rock Creek Nature Center's 12 miles of parkland, hills, and trails are the ultimate escape from the city. Run by the National Park Service, the park schedules a plethora of ranger-led programs for children three and up, including many educational hikes and walks. Budding botanists and biologists enjoy exploring the park's plant life and small critters. Children can learn about the stars at the planetarium. The Nature Center and Planetarium are both closed on Monday and Tuesday.

ZOO

The National Zoo

3001 Connecticut Ave., NW (between Cortland Place and Cathedral Avenue)
(202) 633-4800
www.nationalzoo.si.edu

The 163-acre National Zoo is home to an eye-popping collection of wildlife. No visit is complete without stopping by the zoo's most famous and adorable residents Mei Xiang, Tian Tian, and Tai Shan—the giant pandas. If you're lucky you might catch a glimpse of an orangutan scampering across the ropes high above your head, or get a close-up look at the newest gorilla or elephant babies. In addition to many animals you'd expect to see at the zoo (zebras, tigers, monkeys, turtles, and snakes), there are some unusual creatures that shouldn't be missed, including the giant anteater, the mole rat, and the hardworking black-tailed prairie dogs. Budding zoologists get a kick out of the "How Do You Zoo" exhibit, in which children get to try out different zoo jobs. Be sure to stop by the children's zoo to pet a variety of barnyard friends, and stay a while in the Pizza Park, a playground consisting of a huge rubber pizza pie and fun, shaped toppings.

HEALTH INSURANCE

D.C. Healthy Families
(888) 557-1116 (information)
(202) 639-4030 (enrollment)
www.providers-dchealthyfamilies.com

The Catch Income restrictions apply.

FAMIS—Virginia Children's Health Care Program
(866) 873-2647
www.famis.org

Maryland Children's Health Program
(800) 456-8900
www.dhmh.state.md.us/mma/mchp

The Children's Health Insurance Program (CHIP) is a state and federal program that provides comprehensive coverage for children under nineteen and pregnant women. To join the program you must be a resident and meet specific income guidelines. Washington, D.C., Virginia, and Maryland all do the math slightly differently, but your family's yearly income cannot exceed 200 to 300 percent of the Federal Poverty Level (FPL), which for a family of four would be between $44,000 and $62,000. If you're eligible, the program provides free health insurance for your children, pregnant women, and possibly other family members (depending on each program). The income guidelines change every year along with the FPL.

EDUCATION:
CENTS-LESS SMARTS

"Talk is cheap – except when Congress does it."
— CULLEN HIGHTOWER

From top-ranked colleges to technical schools, from the GED to a PhD, from continuing education to just-for-fun classes, if you can think of it, you can learn it in Washington. Many classes are offered completely free of charge and with no catch, while others can be had for nothing (or next to nothing) if you volunteer your time instead. Volunteers work in school administrative offices, studios, or classrooms, and your work hours are exchanged for classroom hours. The math for these exchanges is spelled out in each listing, but always check with the school to confirm these details. The economics of these work-study programs can change over time.

FOOD & DRINK

Culinary Historians of Washington, D.C.
Bethesda-Chevy Chase Services Center
4805 Edgemoor Lane, Bethesda, MD
(301) 320-6979
www.chowdc.org

The Culinary Historians of Washington, D.C., take food seriously. This membership organization holds meetings open to the public on the afternoon of the second Sunday of the month. These meetings include food seminars with a historical and intellectual bent, from "How Chemistry Facilitated Colonial Food Preservation" or "How Argonauts Ate: Details from Gold Rush Diaries" to the histories of popcorn, hamburgers, tomatoes, and spices. Their Web site is also a good source for other food talks and events around D.C.

For the Love of Food
20 Clarks Lane (off exit 7 of US 795)
Reisterstown, MD
(443) 865-0630
www.fortheloveoffood.com

The Catch Work as a kitchen assistant to take free classes.

Reisterstown may be an hour outside of D.C., but veteran chef Diane Bukatman of For the Love of Food makes it well worth the effort. Bukatman, a graduate of the Culinary Institute of America, has worked as a chef and pastry chef for more than twenty years at exclusive restaurants such as Le Cirque in New York and has taught at the French Culinary Institute. The center offers classes in everything from sushi to Latin cuisine to ice cream and cooking techniques. Working as a volunteer kitchen assistant, you work closely with the chef, pick up extra tips and techniques, take part in classes, and enjoy the scrumptious meal afterwards. For every three classes you assist in, you can attend a class for free.

GiraMondo Wine Adventures

Various locations
(301) 841-7609
infos@giramondowine.com
www.giramondowine.com

The Catch Volunteer pourers attend classes and festivals for free.

GiraMondo schedules cultural and culinary festivals throughout the year. Many of its classes take place at the embassies of wine-producing countries, and the wines are accompanied by food. Volunteer pourers are asked to commit to at least one event a month and dress appropriately for the events (black and white or business casual). To volunteer, e-mail the shop two to three weeks in advance.

L'Academie de Cuisine

5021 Wilson Lane (at Cordell Avenue)
Bethesda, MD
(301) 986-9490
www.lacademie.com

The Catch Work as a kitchen assistant to attend classes for free.

Slice and dice your way to free cooking classes. L'Academie de Cuisine is the largest recreational and professional cooking school in the D.C. area with more than fifty classes a month in which you learn new cooking techniques and cuisines from around the world. Try *The French Cooking Experience, Springtime Chocolates, Basic Knife Skills,* or *Cake Decorating 101,* or take a wine or baking class. Kitchen assistants begin working an hour before a class by prepping ingredients, then nibble their way through the class, and clean the kitchen after the class is over. To join L'Academie's crew of kitchen assistants, you need to attend an orientation and commit to assist on a regular basis (once a week, once a month). Besides attending these classes for free, assistants earn one half-price class for every class they assist in. Full-price classes run about $75 each.

Sur la Table
1101 South Joyce St. (Pentagon Row)
Arlington, VA
(703) 414-3580
www.surlatable.com

The Catch Work as a kitchen assistant to be paid to attend classes.

This gourmet store has everything you need to stock your dream kitchen, including the know-how, and offers cooking classes in everything from ethnic food to baking and technique. You can attend these classes as a teaching assistant and even get paid for your time. It may be minimum wage, but it's better than paying close to $90 a class. Sur la Table is looking to add new kitchen assistants, but the store asks that you make a weekly commitment to work. As a kitchen assistant you will need to show up about an hour and a half before the class to help set up the kitchen, slice and dice ingredients, and help clean up afterward. Sur la Table feeds its assistants and offers employee discounts of 40 percent on products and 50 percent on classes.

Washington Wine Academy
Various locations
(703) 971-1525
JimBarker@WashingtonWineAcademy.org
www.washingtonwineacademy.org

The Catch Volunteer as a pourer to attend classes for free or half price.

Washington Wine Academy has a mix of purely recreational classes and professional-level Wine & Spirit Education Trust (WSET) certification classes. Volunteer to be a pourer to attend any of the recreational classes or events for free, including wine and beer tastings and bus trips to wineries. If you take your Shiraz seriously, volunteer to be a teaching assistant and take the WSET classes for half price. Volunteers and teaching assistants generally have to show up early to the classes, help set up before, and clean up after. Teaching assistants need to make a firm commitment to attend all classes. To volunteer, e-mail Jim Barker, who runs the academy.

Williams-Sonoma

Arlington, VA, Pentagon, 1100 South Hayes St. (between 15th Street and Army Navy Drive); (703) 416-6700

Arlington, VA, Clarendon, 2700 Clarendon Blvd. (at N Bryan Street); (703) 248-8150

5300 Wisconsin Ave., NW (at Western Avenue); (202) 237-1602

Alexandria, VA, Old Town, 825 South Washington St. (between Jefferson and Green Streets); (703) 836-1904

McLean, VA, Tyson's Corner, 8006 Tyson's Corner Center (off Leesburg Pike); (703) 917-7832

www.williams-sonoma.com

While this is clearly not the place for a Cheap Bastard to shop for his or her pots and pans and sea salt, it's a great place to learn how to make the most of that Le Creuset Dutch Oven you picked up at a yard sale for two bucks. On most Sunday mornings (usually two to three times a month) Williams-Sonoma holds free cooking-technique classes with a seasonal spin, from grilling to ice cream to Christmas cookies to Thanksgiving sides. Registration is required.

Learn-a-Palooza!

If you've always wanted to be a burlesque performer or teach philosophy to 1st graders, **Learn-a-palooza** is a one-day event every spring that offers more than 75 free classes. Most classes are held in Dupont Circle and Adams Morgan but spill into other D.C. neighborhoods. The classes include some truly useful lessons (computer classes, foreign language crash courses, finances, car repair, yoga, and fitness), but you can also always count on some ethereal offerings as well ("How to Be Good without God," "How to Change Something in Your Life," "Forgiveness and Compassion Meditation") and of course a smattering of off-the-wall options ("How to Find Gay Men in the City: A Fag Hag's Guide to D.C."). Check out www.learnapaloozadc.com.

ARTS

Art Glass Center at Glen Echo
7300 MacArthur Blvd. (at Benalder Drive)
Glen Echo, MD
(301) 634-2273
www.artglasscenteratglenecho.org

The Catch *Volunteer as a studio manager for free studio time.*

If you have experience in fused glass, the Art Glass Center uses volunteer studio managers to keep things organized and tidy in return for free use of the studio, kiln, and facilities on the day you're in the studio. You need to commit to working at least one Saturday a month. The positions are coveted, so you may be on a waiting list.

DC Glassworks
5346 46th Ave. (between Lafayette Place and Ingraham Street)
Hyattsville, MD
(301) 927-8271
info@dcglassworks.com
www.dcglassworks.com

The Catch *You must volunteer for twenty hours in the studio, then you get one hour of class or studio time for every three hours of work.*

Washington's largest public glassblowing facility, DC Glassworks offers glassblowing classes for beginners to professionals. Volunteer for twenty hours to obtain free classes or studio time. Depending on their skill level or experience, volunteers can expect to do anything from making wax molds or welding to sweeping up the shop. No glassblowing experience is required.

Fairfax County Park Authority
Audrey Moore REC Center
8100 Braddock Rd.
Annandale, VA
(703) 321-7081
www.fairfaxcounty.gov/parks

The Catch *Volunteer for a free class (the math: volunteer at least thirty-two hours to be eligible, then at least eight hours a week).*

Libraries with Class!

Libraries offer free classes, lectures, workshops, and events every week, and for most classes, you don't even need to be a resident of that county or city. Here is a listing of the area library systems and a sampling of the classes they offer.

Washington, D.C., Public Library: www.dclibrary.org

Alexandria, VA: www.alexandria.lib.va.us

Arlington Public Library, VA: www.arlingtonva.us/Departments/Libraries/LibrariesMain.aspx

Fairfax County, VA: www.fairfaxcounty.gov/library

Montgomery County, MD: www.montgomerycountymd.gov/Content/Libraries

Prince George's County, MD: www.pgcmls.info

Computer classes

Book clubs

Films

Health Literacy

Qigong

GED Preparation

American Sign Language

Tech Literacy

Create Your Own Zine

Using MS Word

Aerobics

English as a Second Language

HTML Basics

Poetry

Tango

Concerts

Story times

Game nights

Job Hunting Skills

Small Business Development

Gardening

PowerPoint

Spanish Conversation

Chess

Irish Dance

Scientific Brain Benders

Arts & Crafts

Emergency Preparedness

Astronomy

How to Use Ebay

Advanced Excel

Knitting & Needle-work

Creative Writing

U.S. Foreign Policy

Financial Planning

Meditation

Genealogy

Green Energy and Technology

Web Safety for Teens and Adults

Resume Writing

Building Great Relationships

Collage Art

Writing for Children

Writing Your Memoirs

Social Security Workshop

Health Literacy Online

Interviewing Skills

One-on-One Internet Training

Beaded Necklace Making

Scrapbooking

Decorating on a Shoestring Budget

Landlording

The Fairfax County Park Authority has a huge volunteer program that allows people to take one free class a quarter. It offers classes in everything from athletics to zoom photography, and the arts and crafts classes are extensive. Volunteer a minimum of thirty-two hours and commit to working at least eight hours a week to get free classes. Volunteers sit at the front desk at the recreation centers or assist in the administrative offices. Volunteers at the rec centers are allowed free use of the center they work at.

Glen Echo PhotoWorks
7300 MacArthur Blvd.
Glen Echo, MD
(301) 634-2274
www.glenechophotoworks.org

The Catch Work as a teaching assistant to attend classes for free.

Glen Echo PhotoWorks has taught photography classes to the community for more than thirty-five years. PhotoWorks teaches darkroom techniques in about a third of its classes; the rest are digital. If you're interested in working as a teaching assistant to attend classes for free, give them a call or stop by to set up an interview. Assistants are need in the darkroom.

Hinckley Pottery
1707 Kalorama Rd., NW (between Ontario and 17th Street)
(202) 745-7055
www.hinckleypottery.com

The Catch You must take one class as a paying student before joining the work-study program (the math: three hours of work = one two-and-a-half-hour class).

Hinckley Pottery is a studio and gallery at which you can volunteer in order to get free classes. The studio requires you to be a paying student for one ten-week session (about $350) before you can join the work-study program.

Public Access TV Training and Facilities
DCTV, 901 Newton St., NE (between 9th and 10th Streets); (202) 526-7007; www.dctvonline.tv
Arlington Independent Media, 2701-C Wilson Blvd. (at N. Danville Street); (703) 524-2388; www.arlingtonmedia.org
Montgomery Community Television, 7548 Standish Place, Rockville, MD; (301) 424-1730; www.mct-tv.org

The Catch Classes charge a fee.

These organizations administer Public Access for Cable TV services in Washington, Montgomery County, and Arlington. The federally mandated obligation of cable TV is to provide a channel for any resident to exercise his or her First Amendment right of freedom of expression. Students learn how to operate production equipment (video production, studio production, editing, audio, basic lighting, digital video and editing, etc.). Classes aren't free but are fairly inexpensive. Avid editing classes that might cost $1,500 at other schools will run from $85 to $150 at these training centers. Anything you produce during the public access class or at their facilities must air on that public access channel. All equipment and facilities are provided free or at a discount. Volunteer to lower the cost of classes and equipment.

Smithsonian American Art Museum
8th and F Streets, NW
(202) 633-1000
www.americanart.si.edu

Explore the Smithsonian American Art Museum's collection more thoroughly during its weekly sketching workshop on Tuesdays at 3 p.m. at the Luce Foundation Center. Bring your sketchbook and pencils, and art will supply the inspiration and instruction. The museum also offers a vast array of other free activities, including talks, performances, children's activities, and scavenger hunts.

Washington Glass School
3700 Otis St. (between Oak Street and Wells Avenue)
Mt. Rainier, MD
(202) 744-8222
www.washingtonglassschool.com

The Catch Work as a teacher's assistant for free classes.

Let's Get Physical
Work up a sweat in free classes, from aerobics to Zen yoga, at city recreation centers, local stores, parks, yoga studios, and even public libraries. You will find an extensive list of classes in the Fitness & Fun chapter on page 150.

The Washington Glass School is a large studio and organization that offers a complete array of glass classes, from casting and neon to art glass, metal, and photography. The school doesn't offer glassblowing classes. Become a teacher's assistant to take a class for free. You must commit to a regular schedule helping around the studio. The school is looking for people who are passionate about the work and the studio.

FOREIGN LANGUAGE

Alliance Française de Washington
2142 Wyoming Ave., NW (between Connecticut Avenue and 23rd Street)
(202) 234-7911, ext. 14
www.francedc.org

The Catch Volunteer in the library for four hours a week for free classes and tickets to events.

The Alliance Française has the most extensive array of French language classes in the area. Volunteers work in the library reshelving books or performing administrative duties and translations. Volunteers must commit to at least four hours a week to be eligible for a free class. Once you've completed twenty hours, you can sign up for a class. Volunteers also receive free tickets to movies, performances, and other events at the center.

Global Language Network
GWU Foggy Bottom campus, Marvin Center
800 21st St., NW (between H and I Streets)
(202) 994-8624
www.thegln.org

The Catch $100 fully refundable deposit required to reserve a spot in a class.

Sometimes you come across a free opportunity and you think it's too good to be true. At the Global Language Network you can take classes in almost any language for free. The Network sets out to match native speakers and interested students with the pure aim of "bringing communities together through cross-cultural communication." Classes vary semester to semester, but a typical semester has more than 45 classes in everything from Albanian to Armenian, including more popular choices such as Spanish and French. The center teaches two types of classes: Survival Skills, which are short-term classes that concentrate on basic conversational exchanges; and Immersion, which are semester-long classes that generally meet once a week for two hours. To take an immersion class, put down a $100 deposit to register for the class. The money is fully refundable at the end of the semester as long as you haven't missed more than three sessions during the term. The French and Spanish classes do fill quickly, but many of the others, including Arabic and Chinese, have space.

MEDITATION

Mindfulness Dupont
Foundry United Methodist Church, 1500 16th St., NW (at P Street)
Wednesdays at 7 p.m.
Josephine Butler Parks Center, 2437 15th St., NW (near Euclid)
Thursdays at 7:30 p.m.
(202) 588-9144
www.mindfulnessdupont.org

A group of experienced teachers leads these meditation sittings on Wednesday nights at Foundry Methodist Church and Thursday nights at the Josephine Butler Parks Center. Occasionally, the Wednesday-night sitting turns into a more formal five-week Introduction to Mindfulness Meditation class.

Shambhala Meditation Center of Washington, D.C.
3520 Connecticut Ave., NW (between Ordway and Potter Streets)
(202) 787-1526
www.shambhala.org
The Catch They appreciate donations; yeah, you know, that old karma thing.

The Shambhala Meditation Center offers meditation classes and open meditations on Tuesdays and Thursdays at 7 p.m. and Sundays from 9 a.m. to noon. After the meditation class on Thursday evenings, the center hosts free lectures and light refreshments. Once a month or so, the center offers introductory workshops on Wednesday nights and asks for a voluntary $20 donation. If you are more serious about your meditation or want to further explore Shambhala Buddhism, the center offers many other classes and workshops, some of which are free.

Willow Street Yoga
6930 Carroll Ave., Suite 100
Takoma Park, MD
(301) 270-8038
www.willowstreetyoga.com

The Catch No charge, but they hope you will remember the spirit of Dana (generosity) when they pass the basket.

Willow Street Yoga offers a number of free classes each week, including a Vipassana meditation class on Sunday evenings at 7. The class includes chanting, instructions, and a Dharma talk. If you want to get a double dose of chanting, show up at 6 to take part in the free Gayatri Mantra session. If you're looking to get a little sweaty, check out the free yoga class on Saturdays at 12 p.m.

TALKING HEADS: POLITICS, POLICY, PROSE, AND POETRY

American Enterprise Institute
1150 17th St., NW (at M Street)
(202) 862-5800
www.aei.org

If you liked the Bush administration, you'll love this place. AEI is one of the top conservative think tanks in D.C. and has become the driving force behind the neocon movement. Each week the institute coordinates panel discussions and talks with high-profile conservative leaders and journalists, and you can always find a nice breakfast or lunch spread at these events. Reservations are recommended.

Brookings Institution

1775 Massachusetts Ave., NW (between 17th and 18th Streets)
(202) 797-6105
www.brookings.edu

Brookings is one of the oldest liberal think tanks in D.C. It has a full schedule of public talks and panel discussions on domestic and international policy with leading scholars, political leaders, and journalists. Some of these events can get a bit wonky, but most are accessible to the public. If you do find your head spinning from the finer policy points, head over to the refreshments table to snag free cookies or bagels. Reservations are recommended.

Busboys and Poets

2021 14th St., NW (at V Street); (202) 387-7638
1025 5th St., NW (at K Street); (202) 789-2227
Arlington, VA, 4251 South Campbell Ave. (Shirlington Village); (703) 379-9757
www.busboysandpoets.com

Arguably the best left-leaning restaurant/bookshop/coffeehouse/fair-trade market/concert hall/poetry space/movie theater in town. Busboys and Poets is a gathering place for people to discuss social justice; work toward peace; or enjoy poetry, music, readings, or performances over a falafel or veggie burger.

Center for American Progress

1333 H St., NW, 10th Floor (between 14th Street and New York Avenue)
(202) 682-1611
www.americanprogress.org

The Center for American Progress is unabashedly liberal. *Time* magazine noted that under the Obama administration "no group in Washington will have more influence at this moment in history." The center hosts panel discussions and talks every week on domestic and international issues, such as the environment, labor policy, health care, immigration, and, most importantly, why the conservatives are always wrong. Light refreshments are served, and reservations are required.

Get a Job, Get a Degree

Washington, D.C., and its surrounding counties are home to a number of major public and private universities and small colleges and technical schools. Like any business, these schools need a large support staff. From office assistants and administrative staff to maintenance and mailroom clerks, the universities offer employees reduced tuition. So instead of paying George Washington University as much as $40,000 a year for that graduate degree, why not have them pay you for your time? Forget about paying the University of Maryland almost $20,000 a year to become a computer systems analyst. Take advantage of the system to get it for nothing. Salaries at the schools vary, but most aren't high. However, this perk can make them profitable positions. Here are some Web sites to start your search:

American University: www.american.edu/hr
Catholic University: http://humanresources.cua.edu
George Mason University: http://hr.gmu.edu
George Washington University: www.gwu.edu/employment.cfm
Georgetown University: www.georgetown.edu/working.html
Howard University: www.hr.howard.edu
University of Maryland: www.uhr.umd.edu
HigherEdJobs.com: www.higheredjobs.com

Dumbarton Oaks Museum

1703 32nd St., NW (between S and R Streets)
(202) 339-6410
www.doaks.org/museum

Soak in the elegant surroundings of the Harvard-owned Dumbarton Oaks Museum while you listen to lectures by art scholars from Harvard and other esteemed institutions. The free lectures take place once or twice each month at 5:30 p.m. in the mansion's ornate music room (see schedule on their Web site). Reservations are required.

Heritage Foundation

214 Massachusetts Ave., NE (between 2nd and 3rd Streets)
(202) 546-4400
www.heritage.org

If you prefer your conservative ideology served up Ronald Reagan–style, this is the place for you. Heritage is a think tank "whose mission is to formulate and promote conservative public policies." Every week it invites noted conservative intellectuals, politicians, and journalists for talks and panel discussions. Enjoy tasty sandwiches and refreshments at these events. Reservations are recommended.

The Kalb Report

National Press Building
529 14th St., NW (at F Street)
(202) 994-8266
www.kalb.gwu.edu

Veteran journalist and scholar Marvin Kalb moderates public affairs forums with leading journalists and political leaders four times a year in the spring and fall. The series is broadcast on public TV stations across the country and has featured such panelists as Katie Couric, Walter Cronkite, Secretary of State Hillary Clinton, former Secretary of Defense Donald Rumsfeld, and Nobel Prize–winner Elie Wiesel.

National Academy of Sciences

2101 Constitution Ave., NW (at C Street)
(202) 334-2436
www.nasonline.org

About once a month the National Academy of Sciences presents scientific lectures, readings, and performances by leading scientists, academics, and intellectuals.

New America Foundation

1899 L St., NW, Suite 400 (between 18th & 19th Streets)
(202) 986-2700
www.newamerica.net

One of the newer think tanks to join the ranks of heady policy wonks in D.C., the New America Foundation calls itself "pragmatic progressives" and has a particular interest in foreign, fiscal, and health policy. During any given week you can find talks, discussions, and panels on such subjects as "The Future of Journalism," "Lost in Transitions: U.S. Nuclear Policy" and "American Perceptions of an Arab-Israeli Peace." Most events are open to the public, and you can always depend on a nice spread for breakfast and lunch or even hors d'oeuvres, depending on the time of the event. Reservations are recommended.

Politics and Prose Bookstore
5015 Connecticut Ave., NW (between Nebraska Avenue and 36th Street)
(202) 364-1919
www.politics-prose.com
www.moderntimescoffeehouse.com

Any major political figure, journalist, or novelist who pens a book will eventually make his or her way to the lectern at this bookstore and coffeehouse that has become a D.C. institution. Politics and Prose hosts at least one reading a day. Check out Modern Times Coffee House, the bookstore's coffeehouse, for a full schedule of performances by local musicians and poets.

Rumi Forum
1150 17th St., NW, Suite 408 (at S Street)
(202) 429-1690
www.rumiforum.org

This think tank holds discussions and talks about spirituality and religion. Most events are held at noon, and a free light lunch is provided.

University of Maryland
College Park, MD
(301) 314-7777
www.freestuff.umd.edu

Check out the Free Stuff Web site to see a list of free talks and lectures held at the sprawling UMD–College Park campus. From lectures on international relations or physics to talks by visiting scholars and even celebrities, everything is open to the public.

ODDS & ENDS

City Bikes
Adams Morgan, 2501 Champlain St., NW (at Euclid Street); (202) 265-1564
Chevy Chase, MD, 8401 Connecticut Ave. (at Chevy Chase Lake Drive); (301)
652-1777
www.citybikes.com

Keep your bike on the road by taking free bicycle repair classes at City Bikes.
The shop mechanic teaches everything a biker needs to know, from changing
tire tubes and adjusting brakes to the secret language of tire pressure. Once
you know how to take care of your bike, City Bikes loans tools to keep it in
shape for free. Classes are held at both locations on a regular basis.

Small Business Development Centers
Howard University, 2600 6th St., NW, Room 128 (at Georgia Avenue & Fair-
mont Street); (202) 806-1550
University of the District of Columbia, 4340 Connecticut Ave., NW, Suite
507-B (at Yuma Street); (202) 274-7030
Anacostia Economic Development Corporation, 1800 Martin Luther King, Jr.
Ave., SE, Suite 100 (at S Street); (202) 889-5090; www.dcsbdc.org
University of Maryland, College Park, MD, 7100 Baltimore Ave., Suite 400 (at
Guilford Road); (301) 403-0501, ext. 11; www.capitalregionsbdc.umd.edu
George Mason University, Fairfax, VA, 4031 University Dr., Suite 200 (at
South and East Streets), Suite 200; (703) 277-7700; www.virginiasbdc.org

Ready to start your own business but don't know where to begin? The Small
Business Development Centers are here to help. Sponsored by state and federal governments and local universities, the centers guide you step by step
from the start-up process to the end result. The centers continue to offer
assistance for as long as you're in business with one-on-one coaching and
workshops in everything from developing a business plan to financial planning to marketing strategies and day-to-day management. There is never a
charge for any of their services, and most classes and workshops are free as
well.

HEALTH & MEDICAL:
LIVE FREE OR DIE

"Always laugh when you can. It is cheap medicine."
—LORD BYRON

The cheapest way to stay healthy is to avoid getting sick, but sometimes no matter how hard you try, illness creeps up on you. From ordinary checkups to health insurance, taking care of yourself can really add up. Each state and county has an ever-changing array of low-cost insurance programs and services. Depending on the state and municipal budgets, the programs come and go, and the eligibility requirements also change from year to year. Call or check their Web sites. Another strategy to finding free services for specific conditions is to take part in clinical studies. The good news is that D.C. is the home of the National Institutes of Health and major medical schools, so there's no shortage of studies to take part in and receive free or low-cost care that is often cutting edge.

D.C. Region Departments of Health

If you have questions about healthcare services in your area, contact your Department of Health. It will have programs that can point you in the right direction for all kinds of free and low-cost options for health insurance, cancer screenings and treatments, HIV and STD clinics, quitting smoking, drug abuse, mental health, pre- and postnatal services, and health education and wellness classes.

Washington, D.C.: (202) 442-5955; www.dchealth.dc.gov

Maryland: (877) 463-3464 or (410) 767-6500; www.dhmh.state.md.us

Montgomery County, MD: (240) 777-1245; www.montgomerycounty md.gov/hhs

Prince George's County, MD: (301) 883-7879; www.co.pg.md.us /health

Virginia: (804) 864-7660 or (804) 864-7009; www.vdh.state.va.us

Arlington, VA: (703) 228-1300; www.arlingtonva.us/departments /HumanServices/HumanServicesMain.aspx

Fairfax County, VA: (703) 246-2411; www.fairfaxcounty.gov/hd

WHATEVER AILS YOU:
CLINICAL STUDIES

The National Insitutes of Health and medical centers across the D.C. region run clinical trials for almost any condition imaginable from cancer to acne, from athlete's foot to weight loss. Participants are always needed, and all medication and care is provided free of charge. Sometimes, the organizers may even pay *you* to particpate.

Pick a Study, Any Study

To find a study for a particular condition, check out these Web sites:
National Databases:
AIDS Clinical Trial Information Service: (800) 874-2572,
www.aidsinfo.nih.gov
Center Watch: user-friendly consolidated listing by category:
www.centerwatch.com
Clinical Trials Search: www.clinicaltrialssearch.org
National Cancer Institute: www.cancer.gov/clinical_trials
National Library of Medicine: national database of conditions and studies: www.clinicaltrials.gov

D.C. Area Medical Centers:
Georgetown University Medical Center: (202) 444-0381;
clinicaltrials.georgetown.edu
Johns Hopkins Medicine: www.hopkinsmedicine.org/quality
/patients/clinical_trials
Lombardi Cancer Center at GU: lombardi.georgetown.edu
/clinicalprotocols
MedStar Research Institute: www.medstarresearch.org
University of Maryland Medical Center: www.umm.edu/ct

National Institutes of Health Clinical Center
10 Center Dr. (at Rockville Pike)
Bethesda, MD
(800) 411-1222
www.cc.nih.gov
http://clinicalstudies.info.nih.gov

The National Institutes of Health (NIH) Clinical Center conducts more than 1,000 clinical studies at any given time on their Bethesda campus. The NIH tests treatments for cancer, obesity, and depression, as well as many other common and more obscure conditions. If you have a diagnosis for a specific condition, search their Web site to find a study for which you might be eligible.

SAFETY FIRST: **FREE CONDOMS**

D.C. Department of Health
www.doh.dc.gov/condoms

The Department of Health dispenses three million free condoms a year. The unfortunate truth is that D.C. has the highest rate of HIV/AIDS in the country per capita, and the Department of Health is trying to change this. The DOH Web site will also help you get health insurance, direct you to community health centers, STD clinics, etc. The condoms and lubricant packages are distributed via community organizations, health clinics, bars, clubs, and stores throughout the district.

The Metro D.C. GLBT Community Center
1111 14th St., NW, Suite 350 (at Green Court)
(202) 682-2245
www.thedccenter.org
www.dctoolkit.org
www.fc-kits.org

The D.C. government is not afraid to hand out condoms, and the Metro D.C. GLBT Community Center isn't shy about telling you what to do with them.

The center and other community groups and organizations hand out their own branded "Fuk It" or "Tool Kit" condoms in packs of two, with a lubricant as well. Grab some out of the buckets at the front desk at the center or at **Town Danceboutique** (2009 8th St., NW, between Florida Avenue and V Street; www.towndc.com); then check out its Web site for directions that do not leave much to the imagination. The center has plans to donate condoms to many other area bars and clubs.

FITNESS & FUN:
CHEAP THRILLS

"I cannot afford to waste my time making money."
—JEAN LOUIS AGASSIZ

Free time is always a precious commodity in Washington. And of course, there is no shortage of ways to drop a load of cash when you want to take a break from your daily life. But wait! The city offers a huge amount of fun activities that won't cost you much. Whether you're into yoga, running, biking, working out, or just hanging out, here are some suggestions for great destinations, recreational activities, and other ways to take it easy for free in D.C. The schedules change periodically, so be sure to confirm all information before showing up.

PARK IT HERE! **PARKS OFFERING A VARIETY OF ACTIVITIES**

Chesapeake & Ohio Canal
Georgetown Visitors Center, 1057 Thomas Jefferson St. (between K & M Streets), (202) 653-5190
Potomac, MD, Great Falls Visitors Center, 11710 MacArthur Blvd.;
(301) 767-3714
www.nps.gov/choh/index.htm

Back in the 1800s the Chesapeake & Ohio (C & O) Canal was the lifeblood of the communities along the Potomac River Valley, providing jobs, sustenance, and connection to other communities down the canal. Now, the National Park Service runs the canal's entire 185-mile expanse and provides a place to enjoy nature, work up a good sweat, and catch a glimpse of what life was like in the 19th century. The canal runs from Georgetown to Cumberland, Maryland, but the bulk of the recreational activities take place on the first 40 miles of the canal between Georgetown and Great Falls, Maryland. Whether you're looking to take on a challenging hike or ride or just wanting to lie back and have a lazy Sunday afternoon picnic, the C& O Canal affords visitors plenty of free options. Hiking and biking along the towpath is the best way to explore the park. Try the slew of hiking trails from Great Falls, including a popular but challenging hike on the Billy Goat Trail. If you're not ready to take it on yourself, the park rangers lead Billy Goat Trail hikes, and offer a full schedule of other hikes, bikes, tours, and nature walks. All ranger-led activities are free, except the canal boat rides, which cost $5 to go from Georgetown to Great Falls.

Kenilworth Park and Aquatic Gardens
1550 Anacostia Ave., NE (between Ponds and Quarles Streets)
(202) 426-6905
www.nps.gov/keaq

If tranquility and beauty are what you are looking for, this is your destination. A walk through the gardens will calm the most stressed participant, and you'll swear you've somehow landed in the middle of an Impressionist painting. The park offers birding and nature walks, hiking, and gardening workshops.

Rock Creek Park
Nature Center, 5200 Glover Rd., NW (at Military Road and Glover Road)
(202) 895-6000 (headquarters)
(202) 895-6070 (information)
www.nps.gov/rocr

This is where Washingtonians go to get away, without going away. Rock Creek Park is a huge swath of parklands that probably takes up about one-third of the land in Washington, D.C. Spreading out over 1,700 acres, it's more than double the size of New York's Central Park. A good day in the park could include a stop at the nature center to discover the park's natural history and wildlife, traversing hiking and biking trails, visiting the giant pandas at the National Zoo, taking a ranger-led walking tour, birding, playing tennis (the courts in Montrose Park are free), and enjoying a free concert at the Carter Baron Amphitheatre.

RECREATION CENTERS & POOLS

The Departments of Recreation for Washington, D.C., and the surrounding counties operate more than 125 recreation centers with gyms and public pools. A membership at these gyms will cost you a fraction of the price of your local Washington Sports Club or Equinox. A one-year membership costs from $100 to $170 for residents and a bit more for non-residents. Some of these gyms have equipment and amenities that rival the higher-priced sweat factories while others are, well, not exactly state of the art. Most have Nautilus machines, Life-cycles, free weights and dumbbells, and some even offer such classes as aerobics, yoga, tai chi, and boxing. If you want to cool down, check out the centers that have indoor and outdoor pools. Children and seniors will find many activities specifically geared toward them at some centers, and others can enjoy the pottery and PowerPoint classes.

The Catch Some counties charge a small fee for classes in addition to membership.

Here is some basic information on each county's recreation centers. See Appendix C for a full list of recreation centers with fitness centers and public pool locations:

Washington, D.C.

Department of Parks and Recreation
(202) 673-7647
www.dpr.dc.gov/dpr

The Catch Yearly fitness club memberships for residents are $125, $150 for non-residents.

Sixty-one recreation and community centers exist across all eight wards of the district. Many of these centers have free weights, treadmills, and Nautilus equipment. Non-members can enjoy the centers' indoor and outdoor tennis courts, horseshoe courts, computer rooms, and putting green and can also sign up for classes. Stop by one of the centers to get a D.C. One Card. For three seasons of the year, the pools are free for residents and non-residents, but during the summer it costs $4 per use or $130 for the season.

Maryland

Montgomery County Department of Recreation
(240) 777-6804 (general information)
(240) 777-6900 (recreation centers)
(240) 777-6860 (aquatics)
www.montgomerycountymd.gov

The Catch Yearly membership for residents is $150 and $165 for non-residents. Pool memberships are $365 for residents, $405 for non-residents.

Montgomery County has 16 recreation centers with state-of-the-art weight rooms, four indoor aquatic centers, and seven outdoor pools. Most recreation centers also have basketball courts, fitness and sports classes, art and crafts facilities, game rooms, computer centers, and community lounges. Pool fees are hefty, but the county offers lower rates for families, couples, and seniors.

Prince George's County
(301) 699-2255
www.pgparksandrec.com

The Catch Yearly membership fee for residents is $110 and $275 for non-residents. Aquatics memberships are $216 for residents and $264 for non-residents.

Prince George's 40 recreation facilities run the gamut from standard fitness rooms to world-class Olympic-style training centers. All have decent weight rooms, as well as other athletic fields, courts, and classes. The county has three indoor pools and splash parks and seven outdoor pools open only during the summer. Make the trip to the Fairland Sports and Aquatics Center and the Prince George's Sports and Learning Complex (SPLEX). These expansive high-end facilities have Olympic-size pools, indoor tennis and racquetball courts, and huge fitness centers that would put your neighborhood gym to shame. These locations require a separate pricey membership fee (Fairland runs about $200 a year and SPLEX around $500). To use the outdoor pools in the summer, residents must pay $54 and non-residents $66. Pool memberships are only good at the location of purchase.

Virginia

Arlington
(703) 228-7529
www.arlingtonva.us (click on Parks and Recreation, then Fitness Centers)

The Catch Yearly memberships for residents are $170, $485 for non-residents. Pool memberships are $242 for residents and $473 for non-residents.

Arlington, Virginia, has six recreation centers, most of which can easily be mistaken for any top-end gym. Utilizing the latest equipment, each of the centers has personal flat-screen TVs and personal viewing stations in the cardio room, a boxing training gym, a fully equipped gymnastics area, and plenty of fitness and art classes. The city also has three indoor pools they operate for the public at local high schools.

CHI FOR FREE: **YOGA, TAI CHI, & QIGONG CLASSES**

All Souls Unitarian Church
1500 Harvard St., NW (at 16th Street)
(202) 332-5266
www.imcw.org
www.all-souls.org

The Catch Donations are appreciated.

Prepare yourself for a new workweek by making Sunday evenings the most calm and contemplative night of the week with free qigong and meditation classes. The qigong class begins at 5 p.m., and the meditation class starts at 6 p.m.

Boundless Yoga
1522 U St., NW (between 15th & 16th Streets)
(202) 234-9642
www.boundlessyoga.com

Every Sunday afternoon at 2:30 Boundless Yoga welcomes guests to a free yoga class taught by students or recent graduates from the studio's teacher-training program. And if the free yoga class hasn't lined up your chakras, stop by the studio on select Saturday afternoons for free half-hour energy-therapy sessions by Kim Weeks, the owner of Boundless Yoga and a Healing Energy teacher, and her apprentices. This massagelike work aims to release energy blockages with light touch and gentle pressure. Appointments are first come, first served.

Capitol View Neighborhood Library
5001 Central Ave., SE (at 50th Street, SE)
(202) 645-0755
www.dclibrary.org

Forget about pounding the books and exercising your brain—go to the library to get your heart pumping at an aerobics class every Monday and Wednesday night at 6:30 p.m.

Chinatown Cultural Community Center
616 H St., NW (between 6th and 7th Streets)
(202) 628-1688
www.ccccdc.org

The Chinatown Cultural Community Center is a prime destination for freebies in D.C. Every Tuesday and Thursday at 11 a.m., you can learn the soft martial art of tai chi with the almost 90-year-old master Mr. Pei and his associate Jimmy. The center also offers free tai chi and kung fu classes throughout the week taught by the Wong People (see their listing on page 158) as well as ping-pong lessons, free photography classes twice a month, and workshops in feng shui, calligraphy, and brush painting throughout the year.

Flow Yoga
1450 P St., NW (between 14th and 15th Streets)
(202) 462-3569
www.flowyogacenter.com

The Catch Make a donation of any amount to their favorite charity.

Flow Yoga practices what they stretch every Sunday morning at 9, when the class admission fee is a donation of any amount to its favorite charity, Anahata International, a local organization that trains yoga teachers in postconflict countries such as Kigali and Rwanda as a mechanism for healing and social change.

Lululemon Athletica
www.lululemon.com
Georgetown, 3265 M St., NW (between 32nd and 33rd Streets); (202) 333-1738
Logan Circle, 1461 P St., NW (between P and Church Streets); (202) 518-4075
Bethesda, MD, 4856 Bethesda Ave. (between Arlington Road and Woodmont Avenue); (301) 652-0574
Arlington, VA, 2847 Clarendon Blvd. (between N. Fillmore and N. Danville Streets); (703) 807-0539
McLean, VA, Tyson's Corner, 1961 Chain Bridge Rd. (Tyson's Corner Center); (703) 821-1357

These stores sell an array of yoga-centric items, including bamboo yoga blocks and yoga bras, and offer free yoga classes every Sunday. The Georgetown store schedules one to five classes every week in its upstairs studio for those who want a more frequent workout. Most stores also organize group runs one night a week.

The T'ai Chi Ch'uan Study Center
McLean, VA, McLean Central Park; Ingleside Drive and Oak Ridge Avenue
McLean, VA, Saint Luke Parish School, 7001 Georgetown Pike (at Saint Lukes Drive)
(703) 759-9141
www.taichicenter.com

If you happen to walk past the basketball courts in McLean Central Park on Saturday morning at 8, you might spy a group of about forty-five people performing the silent, slow-motion dance that is tai chi. Everyone is encouraged to join the class, especially beginners. From April through October the class takes place in the park, and from November through March the group moves indoors to Saint Luke Parish School.

West End Neighborhood Library
1101 24th St., NW (at L Street)
(202) 724-8707
www.dclibrary.org

Every Monday night at 7, registered nurse Nancy Saum puts her Western medicine aside and leads a qigong class to help you find your chi—at the library.

Willow Street Yoga
6930 Carroll Ave., #100 (between Willow and Maple Streets)
Takoma Park, MD
(301) 270-8038
www.willowstreetyoga.com

Willow Street Yoga welcomes guests every Saturday afternoon to center their breathing and align their bodies at a free Ansura yoga class. Return on Sunday evening at 6 for Gayatri Mantra chanting, a form of verbal meditation, followed by a traditional meditation class at 7 p.m. For one week every few months, the center offers a full schedule of free day and evening classes.

Wong People

Chinatown Cultural Community Center, 616 H St., NW (between 6th and 7th Streets)
Wong People Studio, 218 Florida Ave., NW (between 2nd and 3rd Streets)
Historical Society of Washington, D.C., 801 K St., NW (between 7th and 9th Streets)
(202) 494-3700
www.wongpeople.com
www.ccccdc.org

The Wong People are a group of volunteers dedicated to the art and cultural heritage of kung fu and tai chi. They offer a full weekly schedule of free classes in both disciplines. This is one of the only places in D.C. at which you will find a pure, non-commercial style of kung fu. Children can also partake in kung fu at the same time as their parents. Most classes take place at the Chinatown Community Center or the group's studio.

SPORTING EVENTS

While it may be costly to see the Washington Nationals or Redskins in action, D.C. has no shortage of options for those who might want to save money while enjoying live action. One of the advantages of having so many universities within a javelin toss of downtown D.C. is the chance to see top-ranked college athletes break records and win championships without having to break the bank. While football and basketball games at the schools aren't free, most of the less-popular sports (i.e., the ones you stay up late to watch every four years during the Olympics) are free for regular-season games. Schools do often charge for the playoff or championship games.

American University

Reeves Field (University Avenue & Quebec)
(202) 885-8499
www.aueagles.com

Free admission to field hockey, women's soccer, swimming and diving, and women's lacrosse games. Tickets to most other sporting events range between $3 and $8 a person, except for football and basketball, which are more expensive.

Catholic University
DuFour Athletic Center
3606 John McCormack Dr., NE (between Taylor and Michigan Avenue)
(202) 319-5286
www.cuacardinals.com

Free sports include baseball, softball, soccer, swimming, tennis, lacrosse, track and field, field hockey, and volleyball.

Take Me Out to the Ball Game

What? You can't swing the $325 for the presidential suite at a Nationals game? Well, that doesn't mean you can't make it to the ballpark. **A little-known secret is that you can grab a $5 grandstand ticket to any Nationals game on the day of the game.** Four hundred tickets for each game are only available at the stadium box office (corner of Half and N Streets, SE), so get there two-and-a-half hours before game time. Limit one per person.

If you'd like to get a bit closer to the baseball action, check out the **Clark Griffith Collegiate Baseball League** (www.clarkgriffithbaseball.com). This amateur league is made up of college baseball players who are looking for a boost into the big leagues. Grab a seat in the bleachers and watch raw but talented athletes play baseball. This is baseball at its purest. Many minor and major league players have begun their careers in leagues such as this; Clark Griffith's most recent success story is Red Sox closer Jonathan Papelbon.

The league consists of seven teams who each play forty games in June and July at fields throughout the Washington area. Check out the league's Web site for the schedules of the Beltway Bluecaps, the Vienna Senators, the McLean Raiders, the Fairfax Nationals, the D.C. Grays, the Carney Pirates, and the Arlington Diamonds.

George Mason University

4400 University Dr. (at Ox Road)
Fairfax, VA
(703) 993-3270
gomason.cstv.com

Free sports include swimming and diving, tennis, track and field, and softball.

George Washington University

Multiple venues
(202) 994-6050
www.gwsports.com

Free admission to baseball, soccer, swimming, tennis, softball, lacrosse, golf, and water polo. Tickets to volleyball and gymnastics are $4 apiece. The events take place at different locations around the campus.

Howard University

Multiple venues
(202) 806-7141
www.howard-bison.com

Cheer on the Bison for every sport except football and basketball. Free admission for soccer, swimming and diving, tennis, track and field, lacrosse, softball, volleyball, and even bowling.

University of Maryland

Department of Intercollegiate Athletics
Multiple venues
Terrapin Trail
College Park, MD
(301) 314-7070
www.umterps.com

At UMD anyone can watch softball, baseball (weekday games only), swimming and diving, tennis, track and field, wrestling, field hockey, gymnastics, golf, and, yes, competitive cheerleading for free. The games and matches take place at different venues around campus.

Washington Capitals

Kettler Capitals Iceplex
627 N Glebe Rd. (between Wilson Boulevard and N. Randolph Street)
Arlington, VA
(571) 224-0555
www.kettlercapitalsiceplex.com

If you're tired of watching the Caps from the nosebleed seats, here's your chance to get close enough to feel the ice spray as Alex Ovechkin speeds by. Morning practices held at the Kettler Capitals Iceplex start between 10 and 11 and are free and open to the public. Practice sessions at the Verizon Center are not open to the public.

GROUP BIKE RIDES & RUNS

Washington, D.C., has some of the best parks (Rock Creek Park, Fort Dupont) and trails (C & O Canal) for biking and running in the world. Bike shops, running stores, and running clubs in the area take full advantage of this by organizing a slew of group events every week, many that run throughout the year. Most rides and runs are open to all skill levels. Bike rides have a "No Drop" policy, meaning no one will be left in the dust. Runs break up into smaller groups for those who run slowly and those who are training for the marathon.

The Bicycle Place

8313 Grubb Rd. (between East West Highway and Washington Avenue)
Silver Spring, MD
(301) 588-6160
www.thebicycleplace.com

Meet at the shop Sunday mornings year-round (if it's above 37 degrees) at 8 for a 30- to 40-mile ride that meanders through Chevy Chase and Bethesda to MacArthur Boulevard and ends at Great Falls. Riders looking for a more challenging trek can continue on to tougher terrain in Rock Creek Park.

The Bike Rack
1412 Q St., NW (between 14th and 15th Streets)
(202) 387-2453
www.bikerackdc.com

Whether you're new to biking or ready for the Tour de France, The Bike Rack has a group ride for you. Every Saturday morning at 10, a slowish, introductory ride covers 20 to 30 miles. Serious riders should join the Sunday morning ride that starts at 8:30 and traverses 40 miles at a brisk pace. For hardcore bikers, the shop sponsors three teams with training and team rides every week. Teams are free but have membership requirements. The year-round rides leave from the Logan Circle shop.

Capitol Hill Bikes
709 8th St., SE (between I and G Streets)
(202) 544-4234
www.capitolhillbikes.com

Capitol Hill Bikes hosts two weekly, year-round rides. Experienced mountain bikers enjoy the Wednesday evening rides through Fort Dupont, and more casual riders glide along on the 40-mile Sunday morning rides. Both treks leave from the shop but are cancelled when it rains.

City Bikes
8401 Connecticut Ave. (at the Capitol Crescent Trail)
Chevy Chase, MD
(301) 652-1777
www.citybikes.com

City Bikes leads a 3-mile group ride for families on Saturday afternoons. The ride starts at the shop and ends at a playground in Bethesda, at which the kids can take a turn on the swings or monkey bars. On the return to the shop, everyone enjoys cookies and juice. The ride gets underway at 1:30 p.m. and runs weekly from May to September. Both City Bike locations also offer free bike maintenance classes most Thursday evenings.

Cupcake Ramble
City Bikes
2501 Champlain St., NW (at Euclid Street)
(202) 265-1564
www.citybikes.com

Every Saturday morning throughout the year (weather permitting), Sol Schott, the pastry chef at Tryst, Open City, and The Diner, leads a relaxed bike ride from City Bike's Adams Morgan store through Rock Creek Park to the store's Chevy Chase location, at which Schott lays out a delicious spread of pastries and sweets. The goodies are all free, but if you want to wash them down with anything, the shop has drinks for sale. After the dessert break, it's time to get back on your bike and try to work off a few of those calories.

Fleet Feet Sports
1841 Columbia Rd., NW (at Mintwood Place)
(202) 387-3888
www.fleetfeetdc.com

Fleet Feet Sports hosts a fun 5-mile run every Sunday morning at 9 that traverses Rock Creek Park and the surrounding area, with athletes running a seven- to twelve-minute pace.

Georgetown Running Company
Georgetown, 3401 M St., NW (at 34th Street); (202) 337-8626
Chevy Chase, MD, 4461 Willard Ave. (between Wisconsin Avenue and Friendship Boulevard); (301) 215-6355
www.therunningcompany.net

Both Georgetown Running Company locations host 6-mile casual group runs. The Georgetown runs take place on Wednesday nights at 6:30 and Saturday morning at 9 (8 in the summer). The Chevy Chase runs are every Tuesday and Thursday night at 7.

Lululemon Athletica
Georgetown, 3265 M St., NW (between 32nd and 33rd Streets); (202) 333-1738
Logan Circle, 1461 P St., NW (between P and Church Streets); (202) 518-4075
www.lululemon.com

The two locations of this yoga specialty store stretch beyond their sun salutations to host group runs every week. The Logan Circle run is on Monday nights at 6:30, and the Georgetown run is on Wednesday nights at 6:30. Groups split up to fit your pace and run from 3 to 7 miles.

Montgomery County Road Runners Club
Various locations
(301) 353-0200
www.mcrrc.org

Road Runners is one of the largest running clubs in the country, and it offers a packed schedule of weekly runs to satisfy its large membership, whether you're a walker or a sprinter. Serious runners join track workouts a couple of nights a week, long runs along country trails and bike paths, and other runs almost every day of the week. Those who trek at paces slower than ten minutes can join The Back of the Pack club for its thrice-weekly runs.

Pacers Running Stores
Silver Spring, MD, 8535 Fenton St. (between Colesville Road and Ellsworth Drive); (301) 495-7811
Alexandria, VA, 1301 King St. (at N Payne Street); (703) 836-1463
Arlington, VA, 3100 Clarendon Blvd. (at N Highland Street); (703) 248-6883
Fairfax, VA, 10427 North St. (at University Drive); (703) 537-0630
www.runpacers.com

Pacers Running Stores host fun runs every Tuesday and Thursday night at 7. These runs are social and easygoing affairs and are never longer than 5 miles, with many different pace groups for all skill levels. Most locations also have additional group runs every week, including early morning runs and long runs on the weekends.

Revolution Bikes
Arlington, VA, Clarendon, 2731 Wilson Blvd. (at N. Edgewood Street), (703) 312-0007
Rockville, MD, 1066 Rockville Pike (between Wootton Parkway and Country Club Road); (301) 424-0990
http://revolutioncycles.com

Both Revolution Bikes locations lead year-round (weather permitting) Sunday morning rides for all levels (9 a.m. in Clarendon and 8 a.m. in Rockville). Clarendon also has a number of other rides on weeknights, including women's rides and hill-training rides.

Washington Running Club

3300 Block of M St., NW (at 33rd Street)
wrc03dc@yahoo.com
www.washrun.org

For more than twenty-five years, the Washington Running Club has invited serious runners to join its Sunday morning long-distance run. Routes are usually between 10 and 14 miles long, and the group runs at varying paces.

FURNITURE & HOUSEHOLD GOODS: ONE MAN'S TRASH . . .

"There are many things that we would throw away, if we were not afraid that others might pick them up."
—OSCAR WILDE

You spot them around the city. Some people call them piles of trash, but the trained eye recognizes them as treasure troves. Furnishing your home with recycled items is not only good for the environment, it's great for the wallet. Students, artists, and collectors have long enjoyed rummaging through garbage to find these free treasures. Once you train your eye to spot a prize, you'll be shocked at the high caliber of castaway items some people consider garbage.

Almost anything you need or want can be found on the street. I can't tell you how many times I've said I need this or that, only to come across that exact item I wanted a few days later on the street. You're limited only by your willingness to forage and schlep. Generally, the smaller the item you are in the market for the more effort you will have to put into your search. If you're interested in larger furnishings, the sky's the limit. Who knows what *you* might find. Here are some of my favorite items I have picked up from the street over the years:

Antique Trunks	Desk Chairs	Oriental Rugs
Antique Wooden Milk	Director's Chairs	Ottoman
Crate	Doctor's Office Scale	Plates, Bowls,
Apple Computer,	End Tables	Silverware
Monitor, and Printer	Exercise Mat	Spice Rack
Art Work, Original	File Cabinets	Storage Boxes
Bookcases	Footstool	Telephone
Chest of Drawers	Lamps	Television
Coffee Table	Leather Easy Chair	Toaster Oven
Couch	Ironing Table	Vacuum Cleaner
Decorative Window	Luggage	Wicker Basket
Flower Box	Microwave Oven	Window Screens
Desk	Mirrors	

Here are some helpful rules to live by when you are on the prowl:

Shop in the best neighborhoods: The ritzier areas have better garbage.

Know when the shops are open for business: It's best to do your hunting on the night before a scheduled pickup. Piles of items appear in the late afternoon and early evening. To find the pickup days for a specific neighborhood, call the Department of Public Works (202-576-9004). Here are the pickup days for some of D.C.'s more posh neighborhoods:

Adams Morgan, Logan Circle, Dupont Circle, Georgetown, Friendship Heights, Tenleytown: Tuesday

Penn Quarter, Capitol Hill, Downtown and Chinatown: Monday and Thursday

Chevy Chase: Monday

Cleveland Park: Wednesday

Cleveland Park and Glover Park: Tuesday or Wednesday (depending on address)

U Street Corridor and Foggy Bottom: Tuesday and Friday

When in doubt, don't leave it out: If you're considering an item, take it. Undoubtedly, it won't be there if you decide to return for it. But if you take it and it doesn't fit your needs, you can always redonate it.

Don't be a hog: If you find something that turns out to not fit your needs, set it out on the street immediately. It's tempting to hold onto a great find for future use, but you don't want to clutter an already cramped apartment. It's like ripping off that bandage; do it quickly. And obviously, someone else will pick up the discarded item and be very grateful to you.

A little work goes a long way: Repaint it, refinish it, change the knobs, or reupholster the cushion, and it's good as new.

Clean it.

Enjoy it.

A LITTLE GIVE & TAKE:
DUMPSTER DIVING MINUS THE DUMPSTER AND THE DIVING

Craigslist & Backpage.com's Free and Barter Category
www.craigslist.org
http://washingtondc.backpage.com

Now that you're feeling broke after moving into a new place you found on Craigslist, you might as well furnish the joint through the Web site as well—except forget about forking over any cash. In Craigslist's Free or Barter categories you can find everything you need to set up your new home and live the good life. The Free category is just what it sounds like: Someone is moving, is getting new stuff, or just needs to get rid of something that still has some good life in it, and instead of chucking it into the landfill they want you to have it. Here's a sampling of recent treasures up for grabs in D.C.: two upright pianos, a computer desk, a couch and loveseat set, computers, printers, fax machines, an office copier, and a 2002 Elvis calendar. On any given day, you're guaranteed to find listings for free moving boxes, soil, and plenty of Curb Alerts, letting you know exactly where and what you can snag off someone's front curb. If you have a skill or item you're looking to trade, check out the Barter category. "I'll give you a professional massage if you fix my leaky faucet," "A week in Ocean City, for painting my deck," "Laptop computer for a hearing aid"—you get the idea. Put away the wallet, and start cleaning out your attic. Backpage.com is a clone of Craigslist but not nearly as popular, so there may be less competition for the freebies on the site.

Freecycle
www.freecycle.org

Someone in Georgetown has just upgraded to a brand-new couch and needs to get rid of that oh-so-cozy but slightly shoddy pullout that has seen them through leaner times. You're new to town and your congressman/boss is paying you bubkas, but you need to furnish your new Adams Morgan studio apartment. It is a match made in heaven, but how do we make the connection? Freecycle is the answer. This Web-based recycling group is in existence to empty out your spare closet and fill your neighbor's living room.

All you have to do is go to its Web site and connect to the D.C. group (groups also exist for Bethesda, Arlington, and just about everywhere else in the world). Once you become a member, your inbox will literally be flooded with e-mail offers for stuff (useful and not so) every day. A typical day's offerings can run the gamut from the worthwhile (including furniture, books, appliances, clothes) to the kooky (advice, leftovers, broken glass bottles) to the incredibly specific (2 yards of yellow felt, size 9.5 women's sensible brown shoes, seventy-five small packets of soy sauce). You can even post "Wanted" messages for practically anything you might need. The D.C. list has almost 20,000 members (and counting), so almost anything you need is up for grabs, and anything you want to get rid of someone else wants. Keep your eyes peeled for the occasional Freemeet organized by Freecycle branches. The Freemeet is a flea market without all that pesky money.

Really Really Free Market D.C.
Facebook—Really Really Free Market

Every third Saturday of the month in Dupont Circle, an assortment of items are up for grabs. Now, you won't find anything here to take to the Antiques Roadshow, but you are likely to stumble upon a beat-up copy of a William S. Burroughs book or a pair of holey jeans. If you're lucky, however, you might find a used bike, interesting books, CDs, or vintage tchotchkes.

Take Me I'm Free!
www.takemeimfree.com

The Catch You may have to pay for shipping.

This Web site is similar to Craigslist and Freecycle. People who have something they want to give away offer it up, and if you want it just click "Take Me." Listings aren't separated by city or state, so if you find a doughnut filler that you must have (this was a real listing), you need to pay the shipping charges. The site makes sure that the shipping charges are not inflated by having the "buyer" make the arrangements with UPS or FedEx.

THRIFT STORES

Georgia Avenue Thrift Store
6101 Georgia Ave., NW (at Quackenbos Street)
(202) 291-4013

A longtime favorite haunt for D.C. thrifters, the Georgia Avenue Thrift Store may look a bit long in the tooth, but you can find some funky or useful items.

Ruff & Ready Furnishings
1908 14th St., NW (between N. T Street and N. Wallach Place)
(202) 667-7833

From the outside this story fits its *Ruff* moniker, but get *Ready* to be surprised by the amazing assortment of vintage furniture inside. Ruff & Ready is not a true thrift store, as most of the items crammed into every corner of this labyrinth are from estate sales and auctions. The prices are a step above what you'd find at the Salvation Army or Value Village, but the selection is legendary. Most of the furniture and what-have-you predates The Beatles, with the finer and pricier pieces on the main level and the real bargains stacked up in the basement. Even if you're not in the market for any furniture, a tour through Ruff & Ready is not to be missed. Open Saturdays and Sundays from 11 a.m. to 6 p.m.

Salvation Army Family Store & Goodwill Retail Shop
1375 H St., NE (between 13th and 14th Streets); (202) 396-1809
2200 South Dakota Ave., NE (at 33rd Place); (202) 715-2658
Arlington, VA, 8228 Richmond Hwy. (at Roxbury Drive); (202) 636-4225
Hyattsville, MD, 3304 Kenilworth Ave. (at 52nd Avenue); (301) 403-1704
Manassas, VA, 11201 Balls Ford Rd. (at Ashton Avenue); (703) 686-4607
www.satruck.com
www.dcgoodwill.org

The H Street Salvation Army is the company's only thrift store located within The District. It's a reasonable size, with a smattering of everything you'd expect to find at a local Salvation Army store. If you're ready for a serious thrifting adventure, head to the expansive Goodwill on South Dakota and in

Arlington, or the Hyattsville or Manassas Salvation Army Stores, at which you can spend a week going through racks of clothes and furnishings.

Unique Thrift Store (U) & Value Village (VV)

Silver Spring, MD, Hillandale Shopping Center, 10121 New Hampshire Ave. (at Powder Mill Road); (301) 431-7450 (U & VV)

Wheaton, MD, 12211 Veirs Mill Rd. (at Randolph Road); (301) 962-0600 (U)

Falls Church, VA, 2950 Gallows Rd. (between Lee Highway and Arlington Boulevard); (703) 992-6560 (U)

Hyattsville, MD, 2277 University Blvd. E (between Riggs and Adelphi Roads); (301) 422-2406 (VV)

Suitland, MD, 4917 Allentown Rd. (between Suitland Road and Branch Avenue); (301) 967-0700 (VV)

Landover Hills, MD, 6611 Annapolis Rd. (between 66th Place and Copper Lane); (301) 341-4646 (VV)

www.uniquethriftstoremd.com

Both of these thrift-store chains can be considered the Costco of thrift stores: they're huge, they have a large selection, and the prices are ridiculously cheap. A visit to any one of these stores would be heaven for an avid thrift shopper, but a trip to Silver Spring, where the two stores sit adjacent to each other, is pure nirvana. Each store has multiple aisles of clothes; art; bric-a-brac; furniture; small appliances; pots, pans, and dishes; musical instruments; linens; books; etc. The quality of the merchandise is really unpredictable. You may have to hunt around a bit to find a gem, but with such a large selection something beautiful and unexpected can be found. And if you don't find what you're looking for at one store, you may get lucky at the other. Prices are generally affordable, but pick up an I M Unique card (free at the Hillandale store) to get 25 percent off everything on Mondays and Thursdays.

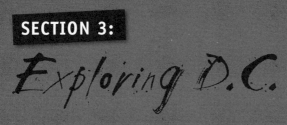

Exploring D.C.

WALKING TOURS:
THE FREEDOM TRAIL

"Afoot and lighthearted I take to the open road,
Healthy, free, the world before me,
The long brown path before me,
leading wherever I choose."
—WALT WHITMAN

Whether you're a visitor to Washington or a local, every building, institution, and neighborhood offers something to discover. The best way to get to know D.C. is to traverse the neighborhoods with someone who knows it well. There is no shortage of free guided tours from leisurely strolls to visits to monuments, government buildings and agencies to nature walks and architectural tours. Sure, you'll visit the Lincoln Memorial, the Washington Monument, and other sites on the National Mall, but many of the tours listed here allow you to venture off the typical tourist trail and discover hidden corners in the nation's capital. Almost every museum in D.C., especially the Smithsonians, offers guided tours on a daily basis. Turn to the Museums chapter (page 201) for more information. Most of the tours listed here take place on a regular basis, while others can be scheduled at your convenience.

GOVERNMENT BUILDINGS

Bureau of Engraving and Printing
14th and C Streets, SW
(866) 874-2330
(202) 874-2330
www.moneyfactory.gov

It won't cost you any money to take this tour, but you'll see plenty of it. This is one of only two facilities in the country that prints U.S. dollars. On this forty-five-minute tour, visitors view the entire detailed process of printing dollar bills from huge blank sheets of paper that end up becoming wallet-sized greenbacks. Along the way, one learns how the process of printing currency has evolved from a six-person operation in the basement of the Treasury Building to a highly complex and elaborate technical process involving hundreds of workers. Tours are conducted Monday through Friday from 9 a.m. to 2 p.m. most of the year but run from 9 a.m. until 7 p.m from April through August. No tickets are required from September to March, but during the high season, free tickets are distributed starting at 8 a.m. You can also skip to the head of the line by arranging your tour through your congressperson's or senator's office.

Eisenhower Executive Office Building

17th Street and Pennsylvania Avenue, NW
(202) 395-5895
www.whitehouse.gov

This grandiose building is the finest example of second-century French architecture in the United States. Situated next to the White House, the Eisenhower Executive Office Building houses most of the offices for the White House staff. Tours are conducted on Saturday mornings but have been temporarily suspended during the building's renovations.

Federal Bureau of Investigation

J. Edgar Hoover Building
935 Pennsylvania Ave., NW (between 9th & 10th Streets)
(202) 324-3447
www.fbi.gov

Tours of the headquarters of the Federal Bureau of Investigation (FBI) have been suspended until further notice. It's uncertain if or when they will resume. Check the organization's Web site for updates.

John F. Kennedy Center for the Performing Arts

2700 F St., NW (at 25th Street)
(202) 416-8340
www.kennedy-center.org

The Kennedy Center is the nation's premier performing arts center, with good reason. A one-hour guided tour of the center takes visitors through the magnificent Hall of States, the Hall of Nations, and five of the center's main theaters, including its three grand performance halls. Along the way, you gaze at works of art, monuments, and structures that were gifts from almost every country in the world. The tour ends with a glorious panoramic view of Washington from the center's rooftop terrace. If you take a tour later in the day, stick around for the free performance on the Millennium stage at 6 p.m. Tours begin every ten minutes from the tour desk in the main lobby and run on weekdays from 10 a.m. to 5 p.m. and weekends from 10 a.m. to 1 p.m.

National Institutes of Health

9000 Rockville Pike (at West Cedar Lane)
Bethesda, MD
www.nih.gov

Tour the National Institutes of Health campus on Mondays, Wednesdays, or Fridays at 11 a.m. Tours begin with a short lecture about the history of the NIH and its current activities and then explores the Hatfield Clinical Research Center. Tours occasionally venture into active laboratories at which you can talk to scientists and learn about their projects. After the tour, take the free shuttle bus around campus and explore the National Medical Library. Reservations are required.

The Old Post Office Tower

12th Street and Pennsylvania Avenue, NW
(202) 606-8691
www.nps.gov/opot

When the lines are too long at the Washington Memorial, head over to the Old Post Office Tower. This self-guided tour leads you through the Bells of Congress, a clock tower, and the 270-foot-high observation deck for what many consider to be the best view of the D.C. area. The tower is open from 9 a.m. to 5 p.m. every day except Sunday, when it's open from 10 a.m. until 6 p.m. During the summer, the tower stays open until 8 p.m., except on Thursday nights, when it's open until 7 p.m.

The Pentagon
Pentagon Visitors Center (Pentagon Metro Station)
(703) 697-1776
http://pentagon.afis.osd.mil

The Pentagon is home to the Department of Defense, the four branches of the military (Army, Navy, Marines, and Air Force), and more than 23,000 workers. It's also the largest office building in the world at almost four million square feet (three times more than the Empire State Building). So be prepared to do some walking.

The sixty- to ninety-minute tour, conducted Monday to Friday from 9 a.m. to 5 p.m., covers about one-and-a-half miles of space. Reservations are required. Groups of five or more individuals should make a reservation at least fourteen days in advance through the Pentagon Web site. Individuals can make reservations through their congressperson's office or embassy.

State Department Diplomatic Reception Rooms
2201 C St., NW (at 23rd Street)
(202) 647-3241
https://receptiontours.state.gov

If it's good enough for the German chancellor or the Crown Prince of Japan, it's good enough for you. Take a tour through these lavish rooms used by the secretary of state, the vice president and other Cabinet members to entertain visiting leaders and dignitaries. Rooms are decorated with a priceless collection of 17th- and 18th-century American furniture and fine art. Tours are conducted Monday through Friday at 9:30 a.m., 10:30 a.m., and 2:45 p.m. and run about forty-five minutes. Submit a tour request at least ninety days in advance.

The Supreme Court
One First St., NE (between East Capitol Street and Maryland Avenue)
(202) 479-3211
www.supremecourtus.gov

You can visit the highest court in the land a number of ways. Courtroom lectures are held every hour on the half hour, from 9:30 a.m. to 3:30 p.m., except when court is in session. On days when court is in session, you can watch the oral arguments by waiting in one of two lines. The first line is for those who want to see the whole session, and the other is for those who want to watch three minutes of the session. The court hosts public exhibitions and shows a twenty-four-minute film about its inner workings. Admission to the lectures is on a first-come, first-served basis, but you can also make a reservation through your congressperson's office.

Treasury, Department of the
15th Street between F and G Streets, NW
(202) 622-0146
www.treas.gov

The Department of the Treasury building was one of the first government structures in D.C., and the huge Greek revival structure is worth a visit. The ninety-minute tours take visitors through meticulously restored rooms. Highlights include President Andrew Johnson's office suite, the ornate Cash Room, and the west dome and lobby. Tours take place on Saturday mornings, and reservations must be made through your congressperson's office.

United States Capitol Building
East front at First Street and East Capitol Street, NE
(202) 225-6827
www.visitthecapitol.gov

No trip to D.C. is complete without a tour of the Capitol Building. It has been home to the House of Representatives and the Senate for more than 200 years, and its rotunda is one of the most recognizable symbols of the American experiment. Tours begin at the Capitol Visitor Center, at which you can see historic exhibitions and watch a film about the building. The tour weaves its way through many nooks and crannies and around the awe-inspiring rotunda, showing visitors many of the famous statues and paintings, revealing unknown stories and facts about the structure. One-hour tours of the Capitol Building begin at 8:45 a.m, Monday through Saturday. Make a reservation online or through your congressperson's office. Check to see if your congressperson's office has staff-led tours. The tour doesn't include a visit to the Senate's or House of Representatives' chambers. To visit the chambers, visitors need gallery passes, available through their congressperson's office as well. International visitors can obtain gallery passes at the Senate or House Appointment Desks on the upper level of the visitor center.

The United States Naval Observatory
34th Street and Massachusetts Avenue, NW
(202) 762-1467
www.usno.navy.mil

The U.S. Naval Observatory houses the master clock, which keeps the official time in the nation, and all clocks follow its example. Tours include information on its timekeeping responsibilities, the history of the observatory (which is also the official residence of the vice president) and a chance to view the night sky through the observatory's 12-inch Alvan Clark refractor telescope. Tours are conducted on alternating Monday nights from 8:30 to 10, and reservations are required. Ticket requests must be submitted through the observatory's Web site at least four to six weeks before the requested date.

The Voice of America
330 Independence Ave., SW (between 3rd and 4th Streets)
(202) 203-4990
www.voatour.com

With an audience of more than 134 million listeners, the Voice of America operates a huge television and radio facility that includes twenty-seven radio broadcast studios, thirty-three production and recording studios, thirty professional audio mixing and dubbing stations, four television studios, twenty-one video editing suites, and one of the largest newsrooms in the world. Tours take place Monday through Friday at noon and 3 p.m. Reservations are recommended.

The Washington Monument
The National Mall (look up, you'll find it)
(202) 426-6841 (information)
(877) 444-6777 (ticket reservations, for a fee)
www.nps.gov/wamo
www.recreation.gov (ticket reservations, for a fee)

The Catch There is a $1.50 fee per ticket for advanced tickets.

This 555-foot obelisk was among Washington's first attractions when it was completed in 1884 and remains one of the most iconic structures in the world. The monument offers visitors spectacular panoramic views of D.C. and beyond. Visiting the monument is free, but you do need a timed ticket. Free same-day tickets are distributed every morning starting at 8:30 a.m. at the Lodge (at 15th Street). During the summer, tickets can sell out quickly, so get in line at 7 a.m.

The White House
1600 Pennsylvania Ave., NW (between 15th and 17th Streets)
(202) 456-7041 (recorded tour information)
(202) 208-1631 (White House Visitors Center)
www.whitehouse.gov
www.nps.gov/whho

Tours of a limited portion of the White House take place Tuesday through Saturday from 7:30 a.m. to 10 a.m., but as you might expect, it takes a bit of work to make it through those heavily guarded doors. Visitors can explore eight state reception rooms including the East Room, in which most presidential press conferences take place.

And while you'll be on a self-guided tour, be sure to chat up the members of the Secret Service who guard the entrance to the Oval Office. These officers know the history behind every room, chair, and painting in the mansion and are happy to share it with you. Tours are only available for groups of 10 or more people and must be requested through your congressperson's office. Submit your request at least thirty days in advance. These tours are popular, so the earlier you put in your request, the better chance you have of getting a reservation.

During the spring, if you're lucky, you can take a tour of the garden and grounds. Tickets are distributed through the National Park Service. And if you have young children, the Easter Egg Roll is the hot ticket. These tickets are distributed through the White House Web site.

NATURE WALKS, HISTORIC HOMES & SITES, **& OTHER TOURS**

Agricultural Research Service
10300 Baltimore Ave. (at South Drive)
Beltsville, MD
(301) 504-9403
www.ars.usda.gov

While you might not think of D.C. as pastoral, it is home to the Agricultural Research Service (ARS), the largest and most diversified agricultural research complex in the world. At any given time, you will find ongoing projects examining nutrition and food safety, animal welfare, crop production, sustainable farming techniques, and how to make the most of our natural resources. On the second, third, and fourth Thursday of every month, the ARS offers tours and talks around the campus. On the first Thursday, the staff discuss the work currently taking place at the center. On the second and third Thursday, the employees load visitors onto a bus for a tour of the expansive greenery. Be sure to explore the ARS Science Hall of Fame and other exhibits at the historic Log Lodge. Reservations are required for the tours; the Log Lodge and Hall of Fame are open during regular business hours.

American Society of Landscape Architects
636 Eye St., NW (between I and K Streets)
(202) 898-2444
www.asla.org

You might not think the roof of a Washington, D.C., office building would warrant a tour, but the American Society of Landscape Architects has transformed theirs into a lush green space that is one of the best examples of environmental roofs anywhere in the country. The idea is to reduce energy use, storm-water runoff, and noise inside the building and to lower the temperature in the surrounding area. The society conducts tours around their 3,000-square-foot garden on Tuesdays, Wednesdays, and Thursdays from 10 a.m. to 2 p.m.

Audubon Naturalist Society
Woodend Sanctuary
8940 Jones Mill Rd. (between Jones Bridge Road and Woodhollow Road)
Chevy Chase, MD
(301) 652-9188
www.audubonnaturalist.org

Every Saturday morning from September through June volunteers lead one-hour birding tours through the lush forty-acre bird sanctuary in Chevy Chase. Don't worry if you don't know the difference between a Carolina chickadee and a yellow-rumped warbler; the friendly staff is happy to teach visitors about the birds that are native to the area. They even lend binoculars if you don't have your own. The society also organizes other extensive walks that take place at various locations in the region every week.

Bladensburg Waterfront Park
4601 Annapolis Rd. (at US 1)
Bladensburg, MD
(301) 779-0371
www.pgparksandrec.com (click on Things to Do, then Nature)

Take a forty-five-minute pontoon boat ride along the Anacostia River with a naturalist. The tour explores the environmental and cultural history of the river and the efforts to clean up and revitalize the waterway. Tours take place Tuesday to Friday at noon and Saturday and Sunday at 5 p.m.

Cherry Hill Farmhouse & Barn
312 Park Ave. (between N. Virginia Avenue and Little Falls Street)
Falls Church, VA
(703) 248-5171
www.fallschurchva.gov

Step back in time to the life of a farmer in the 19th century at this historic farmhouse and barn. The home was built in 1845 for what was once a seventy-three-acre farm. The house is furnished with authentic 18th- and 19th-century furniture, and the hand-hewn barn is well stocked with antique farm tools. On Saturdays during the summer, kids can even get their hands on some of these tools, with an opportunity to peel and grind corn using the vintage machinery. Guided tours of the home are offered Monday through Thursday from 10 a.m. to 3 p.m. and Saturday from 10 a.m. to 1 p.m., April to October. The farm hosts Civil War reenactments, concerts, and festivals throughout the year.

Chesapeake Watershed Eco Tours
Various locations
(202) 686-9813
www.wholenessforhumanity.com

Several times a month, the environmental organization Wholeness for Humanity leads eco-tours to highlight local environmental successes. These tours can lead you to many unexpected destinations, including the Nationals' ballpark, the roof of the Department of Transportation, the National Geographic Building, the Anacostia River, and nearby power plants. Tour leaders make the tours as environmentally friendly as possible. A single tour might have you walking, riding your bike, and hopping on the Metro during the course of the three to six-hour excursion. As the group travels from site to site, visitors often meet the very people who have worked on a green project, so feel free to ask questions. Tours take place throughout the year, usually a couple of times a month. Reservations are required.

D.C. by Foot Free Monuments Walking Tour
15th and Constitution Avenue, NW
(202) 370-1830
(800) 217-7740 (cell phone audio tour)
www.dcbyfoot.com

The Catch Tour guides happily accept tips.

Of course, no trip to D.C. is complete without visiting the monuments and buildings of the National Mall, so every Tuesday to Sunday the guides at D.C. by Foot Free Monuments Walking Tour lead groups on ninety-minute tours around the Mall. The gregarious guides keep you laughing as they explain the off-beat history, symbolism, and architectural details of sites such as the Washington Monument, the Lincoln Memorial, and the Jefferson Memorial. The free tours run at 6 p.m. Tuesday to Friday and at 2 p.m. on Saturday and Sunday from March through November. During the summer, additional times are added. From December through February, the schedule is pared back to a couple of times a week. Meet at the corner of 15th and Constitution, and look for the guide with the baby blue tee shirt and orange hat. No reservations are required. If you can't make it to the live tour, try the free cell phone audio tour.

Franciscan Monastery of the Holy Land
1400 Quincy St., NE (at 14th Street)
(202) 526-6800
www.myfranciscan.org

Just minutes from central Washington, the Franciscan Monastery of the Holy Land was built at the turn of the 20th century with architectural elements that reflect the history of the Franciscan order and the Catholic Church. Tours weave their way through the Byzantine-style church with its detailed replica of the Holy Sepulchre in Jerusalem, deep into the mazelike catacombs to the replica of the Nativity Grotto, and around the meticulously landscaped gardens. Tours take place every hour from 10 a.m. to 3 p.m. Monday to Saturday and from 1 to 3 p.m. on Sundays.

Frederick Douglass National Historic Site
1411 W St., SE (between 14th and 15th Streets)
(202) 426-5961
(877) 444-6777 (reservations)
www.nps.gov/frdo

The Catch The tour is free, but you must pay a $1.50 service charge to make a reservation.

Cedar Hill, Frederick Douglass's spacious Anacostia estate, looks much as it did when the abolitionist lived there. The rooms still display his personal belongings, photos, and gifts from his contemporaries, such as Harriet Beecher Stowe and President Abraham Lincoln. After touring the house, be sure to wander the grounds and take in the view of D.C. from the top of the steps. Guided tours run every day from 9 a.m. to 4 p.m. Tours are limited to fifteen people at a time, so reservations are suggested, particularly during the summer.

Gallaudet University

800 Florida Ave., NE (between 6th Street and West Virginia Avenue)
(202) 651-5050
www.gallaudet.edu

Gallaudet is the world's only university devoted entirely to the education of deaf and hard-of-hearing students. Guided tours focus on the university's history and its role in deaf culture. Savor the school's beautiful grounds, designed by Frederick Olmsted, and its many historic buildings. Students use American Sign Language as they conduct the free public tours. If you don't know the language, interpreters are available. Tours take place at 10 a.m. and 2 p.m., and reservations are recommended. Tours with an interpreter must be requested at least two weeks in advance.

The Music Center at Strathmore

5301 Tuckerman Lane (off Rockville Pike)
North Bethesda, MD
(301) 581-5102
www.strathmore.org

A thirty-minute tour of the Music Center at Strathmore examines the architectural highlights of the building and concert hall. After the tour, visit the lavish Strathmore mansion to see its current exhibition. Tours are conducted Wednesday from noon to 2 p.m. and Saturday from 11 a.m. to 2 p.m.

National Building Museum

401 F St., NW (between 4th and 5th Streets)
(202) 272-2448
www.nbm.org

As you would expect, the building that houses a museum dedicated to exploring all things architectural is itself a wonder. The National Building Museum's glorious Grand Hall, whose Corinthian columns are among the tallest in the world, has been the setting for seventeen presidential inaugural balls. Take a forty-five-minute tour of the stunning space, and don't forget to examine the tops of the massive columns. The tours are offered every day at 11:30 a.m., 12:30 p.m., and 1:30 p.m.

Ratcliffe-Allison House and Pozer Garden

10386 Main St. (between Old University Drive and Old Lee Highway)
Fairfax, VA
(703) 385-8415
www.fairfaxva.gov/museumvc/mvc.asp

Built in 1812, this historic home was one of Fairfax's first residences. Once the home of Richard Ratcliffe, one of the city's founders, it was later owned by Kitty Pozer, a long-time garden columnist for the *Washington Post*. Tour the house and garden, which still lives up to Kitty's high standards, on Saturdays from 11 a.m. to 2 p.m., April through October.

Sixth & I Historic Synagogue

600 I St., NW (at I Street)
(202) 408-3100
www.sixthandi.org

In more than one hundred years, the Sixth & I Historic Synagogue has gone from a traditional synagogue to an African Methodist Church and back to a synagogue again—but a much hipper version this time around. Besides religious services, the synagogue is a popular venue for rock and pop concerts, comedy shows, and lectures by the likes of Condoleezza Rice and Bob Woodward. Take a guided tour on the first Sunday of the month at noon to discover the history and architecture of the building. For a more informal and fun tour, stop by anytime and have Eddy, the Egyptian security guard, show you around.

United States Botanic Garden

245 First St., SW (at Independence Avenue)
(202) 225-8333
www.usbg.gov

At the foot of the Capitol Building, the United States Botanic Garden (USBG) stands as an oasis of calm and beauty. Bring a bag lunch for intimate midday tours of the conservatory or the national garden on Monday and Thursday. One of the staff botanists or trained volunteers walks you through the flora and points out highlights from the garden's collection of rare and endangered species. Once the weather warms up, the USBG also hosts after-work tours of the national garden on Mondays at 5:30 p.m. Throughout the year, the garden also runs many other tours, talks, concerts, workshops, and classes.

United States Geological Survey Headquarters

12201 Sunrise Valley Dr. (between Fairfax County Parkway and Reston Parkway)
Reston, VA
(703) 648-4748
www.usgs.gov/visitors

Erupting volcanoes, hurricanes, earthquakes, and natural disasters—is it the latest blockbuster to hit your multiplex? No, this is the U.S. Geological Survey, the government's natural science headquarters. Take a guided or self-guided tour of the headquarters to get an up-close look at many of the discoveries and subjects studied by the service since its inception in 1879. Exhibits include a large slab of rock with real dinosaur footprints and ancient and modern scientific tools and instruments. Kids enjoy the hands-on scientific activities. Self-guided tours are available Monday to Friday from 8 a.m. to 4 p.m.; two-hour guided tours are by appointment only on Mondays, Tuesdays, and Thursdays.

GETTING AROUND D.C.:
FREEWAYS

"We're gonna go where people pretend to want to go when they can't afford to go someplace good. We're gonna see America. We take no map. We'll follow the sun. Stay in cheap motels and steal what we need along the way."
—AL BUNDY

Making your way around D.C. during rush hour can be a challenge, even if you're willing to shell out the cash. It's ironic that the quickest and easiest ways to travel are also the cheapest and greenest. So leave the car at home. You don't want to wade into the standstill traffic, waiting at red light after red light. Truly, even if it isn't rush hour, you're lucky to go 2 blocks in a row without hitting another red light. And you never know when half the streets will be blocked off for the president's or a visiting head of state's motorcade. To top it off, there is barely any free and legal parking anyway. You'll end up spending a mint on meters, garages, or tickets.

The capital is a walkable and bikeable town. Whenever you can, moving on your own power is the best option. When you can't hoof it, the 106 miles of track and extensive bus systems will get you just about anywhere. While it's not cheap, day and weekly passes can lessen the blow. And for commuting into the city, besides commuter trains and buses, cheap (carpooling and vanpooling) and very cheap (slugging [see page 191] and Smart Bike D.C.) options do exist.

Commuter Connections

(800) 745-7433
www.mwcog.org/commuter2

This organization wants to get you out of your car and onto a train, bus, van, bicycle, or your own feet to get to work. It does its best to make it

---

Carpooling

A number of organizations act as matchmakers for commuters and drivers with extra passenger space. While carpooling and vanpooling aren't free, since everyone contributes to expenses, it certainly keeps commuting costs to a minimum while also being great for the environment. Check out these Web sites for more information:

http://washingtondc.craigslist.org/rid
www.alternetrides.com
www.avego.com
www.goloco.org
www.mwcog.org/commuter2
www.nuride.com

---

easy to do with a number of free programs. Register on the Web site, and the staff shows you the best way to commute by mass transit or the safest bike routes or helps you find someone with whom to carpool or vanpool. The truly amazing program is called "Guaranteed Ride Home." Here's the scenario: You carpool or commute into work one day, but then you have a personal or family emergency. You can't find a commuter train or bus to take you home, so what do you do? Commuter Connections sends a car service to pick you up and drive you to your front door, at no cost. Even if you have to work late and miss your ride, you're covered. The organization limits the use of the free car service to four times a year per person.

Slugging
www.slug-lines.com

Slug Lines of Northern Virginia probably wins the prize for the most unique way to get to work fast and for free. Slugging, or "instant carpooling," isn't run by any one person or organization; it grew organically out of the use of High Occupancy Vehicle (HOV) lanes on the highways leading into D.C. from Virginia. Cars must have at least three passengers to use these speedier lanes, so many drivers, wanting to get to work faster, decided to pick up two or more passengers. Drivers get to use the HOV lane, and passengers get a free and quick ride.

Slugging has been a way of life for commuters for more than thirty-five years and has expanded to many different Virginia and D.C. locations. Riders line up, usually at Park & Rides, and drivers pull up and call out how many passengers they need and the destination ("two for the Pentagon"). Passengers get on board, and drivers drop them off at specific points at the destination.

Smart Bike D.C.
(800) 899-4449
Logan Circle, 14th Street and Rhode Island Avenue, NW (southwest corner)
Dupont Circle, Massachusetts Avenue and Dupont Circle, NW (west of Dupont Circle)
Reeves Center, 14th and U Streets, NW (northwest corner)
Shaw, 7th Street and T Street, NW (northwest corner)
Foggy Bottom, 23rd and I Streets, NW (northwest corner)
Gallery Place, 7th and F Streets, NW (northwest corner)
Farragut Square, 17th and K Streets, NW (southeast corner)

Metro Center, 12th and G Streets, NW (northeast corner)
Judiciary Square, 4th and E Streets, NW (southeast corner)
McPherson Square, 14th and H Streets, NW (northwest corner)
www.smartbikedc.com

The Catch Yearly membership is $40 for unlimited use of bikes.

Smart Bike D.C. puts a kink into all those excuses for not using a bike to get around town. Widely popular in Europe, this self-service bike-sharing system works much the same way in the States. Members pay a small yearly subscription ($40) to have unlimited access to bikes. Bikes are stationed at ten locations around D.C., with plans for more in the future. Swipe your membership card at any kiosk, and the bike is yours for up to three hours. Use the bike to commute around town or just to take a lunchtime spin along the C & O Canal. Return it to any station. Of course, you're responsible for any damage to the bike once you ride it, and if it's not returned within twenty-four hours, you'll see a whopping $550 charge on next month's credit card bill.

Washington Metropolitan Area Transit Authority (Metro)
(202) 637-7000
www.wmata.com

Metro's extensive rail and bus service covers every corner of The District, nearby Maryland and Virginia, and the suburbs. Originally designed to be the antithesis of the New York City subway system—clean, safe, airy, and reliable—the Metro stations are cavernous and easy on the eyes. Fares are based on the distance you're traveling. A short trip costs $1.65, an end-to-end ride, $4.50. Buses charge $1.35 a ride, no matter the destination. But here are a couple of strategies to work the system and save a few bucks. First, get a SmarTrip card, which saves you ten cents a trip, but more importantly, it's your ticket to unlimited bus transfers for three hours for one

Hacking It in D.C.
You won't be surprised by this recommendation. Don't ever take a cab. Besides its being expensive (just hopping into a taxi will cost you at least $5), the wild ride invariably takes longer than grabbing the nearest metro.

fare. The card also saves you fifty cents a trip when you transfer from bus to train or vice versa. Buy an unlimited one-day train pass for $7.80 if you're going to multiple destinations. The only catch is you can't use the day pass until 9:30 a.m. Weekly bus and rail passes are also available and may be a good deal, depending on how much you travel. The Metro connects up with the MARC in Maryland and the VRE in Virginia to make the commuting to the outer suburbs even easier. Trains run from 5 a.m. to midnight Sunday to Thursday and 7 a.m. to 3 a.m. on Friday and Saturday.

GETTING OUT OF TOWN

Auto Driveaway

8143 Richmond Hwy., Suite No. 202 (at Janna Lee Avenue)
Alexandria, VA
(703) 360-8250
www.autodriveawaydc.com

The Catch A $350 refundable deposit.

Forget about flying, Greyhound, or Amtrak—here's your chance to see America the way it was meant to be seen, behind the wheel of your own gas-guzzling, pedal-to-the-metal, "where the hell is the next rest stop?" automobile. With forty locations throughout the United States and Canada, Auto Driveaway provides customers with the free use of a late-model car to practically any major city. Auto Driveaway matches people or companies that need vehicles moved from place to place and drivers who want to get from here to there. Call to see what's available, pay your deposit, and hit the road. Cars are distributed to drivers twenty-three and older with two photo IDs on a first-come, first-served basis. The company gives you time to sightsee by allotting extra time from start point to destination (e.g., four days to Florida, ten days to the West Coast). Auto Driveaway returns your deposit when you deliver your car. The looser your travel plans are, the better the system works. Cars come with a free full tank of gas; additional gas is the driver's responsibility.

Vipassana Meditation Center

Chestertown, MD
Blue Ridge, VA
(202) 521-5203
www.dhamma.org (click "North America", then "Mid-Atlantic")

The Catch Donations of any amount are accepted, but not required, at the end of the ten-day retreat.

Vipassana offers its ten-day silent meditation retreat free of charge (including all accommodations, meals, and instruction) but only if you keep mum about the service. In fact, you will have to keep mum about everything because this is a 10-day silent retreat. No meditation experience is required, and the focus isn't religious. Vipassana believes that technique and practice of meditation is a "remedy for universal ills." Fill out the detailed application at their Web site, and make a reservation one to two months in advance.

GARDENS & GARDENING:
DIRT CHEAP

"Your first job is to prepare the soil. The best tool for this is your neighbor's motorized garden tiller. If your neighbor does not own a garden tiller, suggest that he buy one."
—DAVE BARRY

Washington, D.C., is bursting with blooms, with public gardens large and small scattered throughout the city. From bountiful community gardens to the grand U.S. Botanic Gardens and Arboretum, gardeners delight in some of the most stunning horticulture in the world. Not only can you partake of the sights and smells of the gardens, you can produce some pretty sweet stuff yourself. Cultivate your own plot of land for next to nothing in one of the area's many community gardens, and develop your own green thumb through free gardening classes.

Brookside Gardens
1800 Glenallan Ave. (just off Randolph Road)
Wheaton, MD
(301) 962-1400
www.brooksidegardens.org

Located in Wheaton Regional Park, Montgomery County's fifty-acre garden is packed with a little of everything: an azalea garden, a rose garden, a Japanese garden, a children's garden, a fragrance garden, and two conservatories with lush tropical plants and seasonal displays. Brookside also hosts a popular story time for kids every Saturday morning, and the park is home to one of the most amazing playgrounds this side of Disney World. The gardens are open every day sunrise to sunset; the conservatories, from 10 a.m. to 5 p.m.

Constitution Gardens
Constitution Avenue and 17th Street, NW
(202) 426-6841
www.nps.gov/coga

Just to the side of the National Mall, the Constitution Gardens are home to the Vietnam War Memorial, a small island with a tribute to the signers of the Declaration of Independence, and fifty acres of landscaped grounds and meandering trails.

Green Spring Gardens
4603 Green Spring Rd. (between Braddock Road and Little River Turnpike)
Alexandria, Virginia
(703) 642-5173
http://www.fairfaxcounty.gov/parks/gsgp

Green Spring inspires locals to clear out the trash from their backyards and transform them into lush gardens. Green Spring has more than twenty demonstration gardens of every size on display. So whether you live in a townhouse or an apartment, the center has floral possibilities for you. Examine the children's garden, the herb garden and the tasty kitchen garden. Meander through the twenty-eight acres, but keep your hands off the tomatoes. Green Spring charges for classes and workshops. The gardens are open every day from dawn till dusk.

Kenilworth Park and Aquatic Gardens
1550 Anacostia Ave., NE (between Ponds and Quarles Streets)
(202) 426-6905
www.nps.gov/keaq

A walk along the ponds, with their rare water lilies and the low hum of croaking frogs, will calm the most stressed-out among us. You will swear you have somehow landed in the middle of an Impressionist painting. The park offers birding and nature walks, hiking, gardening workshops, and serenity. Kenilworth Park is normally open from 8 a.m. to dusk but closed when road conditions are hazardous. Kenilworth Aquatic Gardens are open from 7 a.m. to 4 p.m. every day except Thanksgiving, December 25, and January 1.

National Arboretum
3501 New York Ave., NE (at 31st Street)
(202) 245-2726
www.usna.usda.gov

The lush greenery that makes up the 446-acre National Arboretum serves as a living museum of trees, shrubs, and herbaceous plants from around the world. The collections include the miniature wonders of the National Bonsai & Penjing Museum, the dazzling colors of the azalea collection, and the world's largest herb garden, featuring more than 1,500 herbs from around the world. The best way to explore the Arboretum is on bike or by car, if you must. If you're hoofing it, the friendship garden, the herb garden, and the bonsai collection are all within walking distance of each other. Take the $4 tram tours of the grounds for a more in-depth look. The Arboretum's regular events include special art exhibits, gardening workshops, and evening hikes. Most of the events and workshops are free. Open every day from 8 a.m. to 5 p.m.

River Farm

7931 East Boulevard Dr. (off Mt. Vernon Memorial Highway)
Alexandria, VA
(703) 768-5700
www.ahs.org/river_farm

River Farm sits on the banks of the Potomac River and was once one of George Washington's five farms. It's now home to the American Horticultural Society, a twenty-five-acre area that includes a delightful children's garden, beautiful formal gardens, and even a small orchard of apple, pear, cherry, plum, and persimmon trees. The gardens are open Monday to Friday from 9 a.m. to 5 p.m., from April through September, and also on Saturday from 9 a.m. to 1 p.m.

United States Botanic Garden

100 Maryland Ave., SW (between 1st and 3rd Streets)
(202) 225-8333
www.usbg.gov

The Botanic Garden is split into three sections: the Conservatory, the National Garden, and Bartholdi Park. The newly renovated Conservatory acts as a kind of living plant museum and maintains habitats for nearly 4,000 species of flora from across the country. The National Garden features the rose garden, the butterfly garden, the First Lady's water garden, and a regional garden cultivating plants that are native to the mid-Atlantic region. Bartholdi Park is a more classically designed formal garden configured around an impressive fountain. The garden offers guided tours and evening walks, "Mommy and Me" classes, and many other gardening classes and workshops (many but not all are free). Space is limited for these events. Registration is required. Open every day from 10 a.m. to 5 p.m.

GARDENING

When it's time to get your hands dirty, you can find a number of free classes or advice on gardening. The U.S. Botanic Garden, the National Arboretum, and Brookside Gardens (see listings above) offer many free classes, workshops, and lectures on everything from container gardening to landscape design. Here are some other places that will help you dig in.

Get the Dirt

The Department of Public Works has an unlimited supply of mulch and compost that is available for free to every resident of the district. Officially, this is for D.C. residents only, but since nobody is checking IDs, non-residents can take part, too. Compost is called the "black gold" of gardening and is an essential ingredient for any lush window box, houseplant, or backyard vegetable garden.

Although the compost and mulch are completely free, the department doesn't make it easy for you to find it. The pile is kept on a DPW lot, in a rough-looking, industrial neighborhood. The unmarked piles sit on the left side of the entrance along the fence and are crammed in among the parked dump trucks, front-end loaders and snowplows. If you don't spot them right away, don't be deterred. Stop a Public Works employee to point you in the right direction.

Once you find it, shovel yourself a load of this messy but useful, nutrient-rich, organic plant food, and your garden will thank you for it. The lot is open for pickups Monday to Friday from 8 a.m. to 4 p.m. and Saturday from 8 a.m. to 2 p.m.; 900 New Jersey Ave., SE (at K Street), (202) 645-3900.

If you are not quite that adventurous, you can grab free compost to go anytime at your local Starbucks Coffee. Yes, your favorite coffee pusher is happy to give away its used grounds to anyone who wants them. The dark grinds combine with soil to make a perfect blend to wake up any houseplant. Most stores participate in this program, but be sure to call ahead; www.starbucks.com.

Northern Virginia gardeners never have to buy mulch again. You can have wood-chip mulch delivered to your home, free of charge, from NOVEC. Call (703) 392-1661 to set up a delivery. Contact Growing Earth Tree Care, and when they cut down a tree in your neighborhood, they'll happily dice the remains into mulch and deliver it to your house; (703) 818-8228, www.growingearth.com. If you're able to haul it yourself, Fairfax County has eight mulch-distribution sites at which you can pick it up; (703) 324-5995, www.fairfaxcounty.gov (search "free mulch" on the home page).

Department of Parks and Recreation Environmental Education Program

Lederer Environmental Education Center, 4801 Nannie Helen Burroughs Ave. (at 48th Street), NE; (202) 727-8061
Twin Oaks Garden, 4025 14th St., NW (at Taylor Street); (202) 576-3253
(202) 671-0396 (DPR Environmental Education information)
www.dpr.dc.gov (click on Environmental Education)

The district's Environmental Education Program runs classes and workshops throughout the year on gardening subjects such as "Building a Backyard Habitat," container gardening, pruning trees, "Natural Strategies to Combat Invasive Species," and vegetable gardening. These workshops take place at least once a month on the weekends. You are most likely to find these classes at Lederer or Twin Oaks, the organization's two environmental education centers, but they also take place at recreation centers around D.C. If you're ready to start digging but you don't have any land, you can apply for a community garden plot through the department, although there is a long waiting list. The plot costs $25 a year.

Grow It Eat It

Various locations
(800) 342-2507 or (410) 531-1757 (Home and Garden Information Hotline)
www.growit.umd.edu (main Web site)
www.hgic.umd.edu (to submit questions to Master Gardeners)

Grow It Eat It is a program sponsored by the University of Maryland College of Agriculture to take what's been taught in the classroom and spread it around every garden in Maryland, like fine manure. The program assists budding gardeners in raising heirloom tomatoes, fat red peppers, or succulent blue Hubbard squash. Its volunteer master gardeners hold vegetable gardening classes that teach participants how to grow edible plants anywhere: backyards, decks, balconies, or front stoops. If you don't have space, the organization helps you find a plot in a community garden. When you run into problems, call or e-mail the Home and Garden Information Hotline, Monday to Friday from 8 a.m. to 1 p.m. Classes are held in libraries and community centers across Maryland, including Montgomery and Prince George's Counties. Open to non-residents as well.

MUSEUMS:
FREE TO SEE

"I hate flowers. I only paint them because they're cheaper than models and they don't move."
—GEORGIA O'KEEFFE

Washington, D.C., and the surrounding area are awash with world-class museums, and an astounding number of them are free. Whatever your taste or interest, whether it's history, art, crafts, science, archaeology, space flight, historic homes, or the military or government, and whatever your age, background, or curiosities, D.C. has a museum that caters to you. While a few museums appreciate donations, the vast majority are free.

Alexandria Archaeology Museum

The Torpedo Factory Art Center
105 North Union St., #327 (at King Street)
Alexandria, VA
(703) 838-4399
http://oha.alexandriava.gov/archaeology

Dig into the history of Alexandria and the country with exhibits of artifacts from the area, dating back 5,000 years. From prehistoric stone tools to 19th-century medicinal paraphernalia, the Alexandria Archaeology Museum traces the history of the United States. The museum offers free tours of active digs around the city, and you can even participate in the digs yourself by volunteering. Throughout the year, the center offers family activities and dig days, during which the public participates in an excavation for a fee. The museum is located in the Torpedo Factory Art Center, which is home to more than 160 visual artists. Explore the many art studios and galleries in the center. The museum is open Tuesday to Friday from 10 a.m. to 3 p.m., Saturdays from 10 a.m. to 5 p.m., and Sundays from 1 p.m. to 5 p.m. It is closed on Mondays and on New Year's Day, Easter, the Fourth of July, Thanksgiving, and Christmas.

American University Museum

4400 Massachusetts Ave., NW (at Ward Circle and Nebraska Avenue)
(202) 885-1300
www.american.edu/cas/katzen/museum

Based in the Katzen Art Center, the American University Museum showcases more than twenty modern art shows a year. The school often collaborates with foreign embassies to present works by international artists. Open from 11 a.m. to 4 p.m. Tuesday to Sunday and one hour before events at the Katzen Center.

Anacostia Community Museum
1901 Fort Place, SE (between Erie Street and Bruce Place)
(202) 633-4820
www.anacostia.si.edu

Located in the Anacostia area of Washington, D.C., the museum explores and documents the effects of history and modernity on communities world-wide. The museum's definition of "community" isn't limited to geography; it includes ethnic, creative, and handicapped communities and especially the changing dynamics in the local Anacostia community. The museum features temporary exhibitions throughout the year. Open every day except Christmas from 10 a.m. to 5 p.m.

Anderson House Museum of the Society of the Cincinnati
2118 Massachusetts Ave., NW (between 21st and 22nd Streets)
(202) 785-2040
www.societyofthecincinnati.org

The Anderson House is home to the Society of the Cincinnati, an organization dedicated to preserving the memory of the Revolutionary War. Free guided tours weave through the early 20th-century mansion with a focus on the historical collections. Tours run Tuesday to Saturday at 1:15, 2:15, and 3:15 p.m.

Arlington Historical Museum
1805 South Arlington Ridge Rd. (at South 20th Street)
(703) 892-4204
www.arlingtonhistoricalsociety.org

This converted schoolhouse is home to a collection of art and artifacts that explores the history of Arlington as well as the building of the Pentagon. Open Saturdays and Sundays from 1 to 4 p.m.

Arlington House, The Robert E. Lee Memorial
Arlington National Cemetery
George Washington Memorial Parkway
McLean, VA
(703) 235-1530
www.nps.gov/arho

Originally built by George Washington Parke Curtis (GW's stepgrandson) and his slaves to serve as a residence and memorial to his namesake, Arlington

House is now a memorial to another general, Robert E. Lee. Operated by the National Park Service, this grand estate is maintained in the 19th-century style. Guided ranger tours and other family activities are often available, but check with them when you arrive.

Art Museum of the Americas
201 18th St., NW (at Virginia Avenue)
(202) 458-6016
www.museum.oas.org

The Art Museum of the Americas, part of the Organization of American States (a group of North, Central, and South American nations) houses a collection of modern and contemporary art from the thirty-four member states, particularly Latin America and the Caribbean. Reservations are required for free tours of the exhibitions. Open Tuesday to Sunday, 10 a.m. to 5 p.m.

Belair Mansion
12207 Tulip Grove Dr. (between Belair Drive and Foxhill Lane)
Bowie, MD
www.cityofbowie.org/Museum

Drive to Bowie, Maryland, to tour this grand Georgian plantation built in 1745. Belair was once home to two Maryland governors, as well as many others, and remained a private residence until 1957. The mansion's gracious furnishings and artwork reflect its long history. Stop by the nearby Belair Stables, the Bowie Railroad Museum and the Radio and Television Museum for a full day of sightseeing. Open Tuesday to Sunday, noon to 4 p.m.

Belair Stable Museum
2835 Belair Dr. (between Sun Lane and Spangler Way)
Bowie, MD
www.cityofbowie.org/Museum

Until it closed in 1957, the Belair stable had been active for more than 250 years and was the oldest horse farm in the country. During the stable's heyday in the 1930s, it was home to the only sire and son to win horseracing's Triple Crown (Gallant Fox in 1930 and Omaha in 1933). Open Tuesday to Sunday, noon to 4 p.m.

Bowie Railroad Museum
8614 Chestnut Ave. (at 11th Street)
Bowie, MD
www.cityofbowie.org/Museum

While visiting the other free Bowie museums, plan to have a picnic lunch on the grounds of this turn-of-the-century railroad station. Explore railroad memorabilia and vintage Norfolk and Western cabooses. Open Tuesday to Sunday, noon to 4 p.m.

Capitol Visitors Center
First Street and East Capitol Street, NE
(202) 226-8000
www.visitthecapitol.gov

The Capitol Visitor Center is the newest addition to the federal landscape. It serves as the entry way and information center for the Capitol Building and for anyone viewing the Senate or House of Representatives while they are in session. The exhibition "*E Pluribus Unum*: Out of Many, One," is open to all visitors and examines the history of the Capitol Building, illustrates the inner workings of Congress, and gives you a peek behind the scenes with architectural models, artifacts, and videos. Free tours of the Capitol Building are available with a limited number of tour passes distributed at the visitor center. Reserve tickets through your senator or congressperson's office. International visitors can obtain gallery passes at the House and Senate Appointment Desks on the upper level of the Capitol Visitor Center. Open Monday through Saturday from 8:30 a.m. to 4:30 p.m.

Daughters of the American Revolution Museum
1776 D St., NW
(202) 628-1776
www.dar.org

The Daughters of the American Revolution Museum has a collection of more than 30,000 national treasures. Its galleries and thirty period rooms are filled with objects and artifacts from the time of the *Mayflower* landing to the Civil War. Guided tours are available Monday to Saturday. Children five to seven years old shouldn't miss the Colonial Adventure program that takes place the first and third Saturday of every month. It gives children a chance to experience life as a colonial child by dressing in colonial costumes, playing the games of the time and attending a colonial tea party.

Department of the Interior Museum
1849 C St., NW
(202) 208-4743
www.doi.gov/interiormuseum

The main purpose of the Department of Interior Museum is to tout the good works of the department and its bureaus, but visitors learn about endangered animals, wildlife protection, life on an Indian reservation, and pollination. The museum features historic artworks by Ansel Adams and William Henry Jackson, dioramas and interactive exhibits. Tours of the building focus on its architecture and more than two dozen historic murals. Reservations suggested. Monday through Friday 8:30 a.m. to 4:30 p.m. and the third Saturday of the month, 1 to 4 p.m.

Drug Enforcement Administration Museum
700 Army Navy Dr. (at S Hayes Street)
Arlington, VA
(202) 307-3463
www.deamuseum.org

Sure, other museums might have priceless artifacts, but do they have bongs, crack vials, and cocaine toothache drops? The Drug Enforcement Administration Museum tells the story of drugs, drug addiction, and drug enforcement in the United States through unusual exhibits and interactive displays. Open Tuesday to Friday, 10 a.m. to 4 p.m.

Dumbarton Oaks Museum
1703 32nd St., NW (between S and R Streets)
(202) 339-6410
www.doaks.org/museum

D.C. is a great college town, but you may not have realized that a branch of Harvard University exists in the middle of Georgetown. Dumbarton Oaks is an expansive federal-style home that was donated fully furnished to Harvard along with an extensive collection of Byzantine and Pre-Columbian art and works by European masters. Much of the building operates as a research library and an institute for the study of these periods. Learn more about these subjects at weekly lectures held most Thursdays at 5:30 p.m. If you are visiting on Saturday, be sure to take the Historic Rooms tour (Saturdays at 3 p.m.) to get a peek at elegant chambers not usually open to the public. Open Tuesday to Sunday, 2 to 5 p.m.

Fairfax Museum
10209 Main St. (between Locust Street and Old Lee Highway)
Fairfax, VA
(703) 385-8414
www.fairfaxva.gov/MuseumVC/MVC.asp

Located in a historic 19th-century schoolhouse, the Fairfax Museum features exhibitions about the history of Fairfax and Virginia. The museum also serves as a visitor center for the Northern Virginia and D.C. area. You can combine your visit with a trip to the nearby Civil War Interpretive Center at Blenheim. Open daily from 9 a.m. to 5 p.m.

Folger Shakespeare Library
201 East Capitol St., SE (between 2nd and 3rd Streets)
(202) 544-4600
www.folger.edu

Not only is the Folger home to the world's largest and finest collection of Shakespeare memorabilia—including more than half of the first folios still in existence—but the building's Elizabethan-inspired spaces and exhibitions embody Shakespeare's time and works. Exhibitions and tours of the library are free. The library is open Monday to Saturday 10 a.m. to 5 p.m. Tours are given Monday through Friday at 11 a.m. and 3 p.m. and Saturdays at 11 a.m. and 1 p.m.

Fort Ward Museum & Historic Site
4301 W Braddock Rd. (between N. Van Dorm Street and Marlboro Drive)
Alexandria, VA
(703) 838-4848
oha.alexandriava.gov/fortward

Fort Ward is the best preserved of the battery of forts used to protect Washington, D.C., during the Civil War. The museum contains artifacts from that era and traces the history of local battles as well as life in occupied Alexandria during the war. The fort also plays host to Civil War reenactments throughout the year. Open Monday to Saturday, 10 a.m. to 5 p.m., and Sunday, 12 to 5 p.m.

Freeman Store and Museum
131 Church St., NE (between Mill Street and Dominion Road)
Vienna, VA
(703) 938-5187
www.historicviennainc.org

The Freeman General Store served the local community from 1859 to 1920 (with a short break during the Civil War, when it was a Union hospital and hotel) and is currently stocked with more-modern candies and sundries. Touring the store and home gives one a sense of what life was like in the 1800s. The Victorian-style museum showcases exhibits about the area's history. Open Wednesday through Saturday, noon to 4 p.m., and Sunday, 1 to 5 p.m., from February to December.

Freer Gallery of Art
1150 Jefferson Dr., SW (at 12th Street)
(202) 633-1000
www.asia.si.edu

The Freer Gallery of Art, opened in 1923, was the first Smithsonian museum to be dedicated entirely to fine art. Its current collection spans 6,000 years

---

(Day and) Night at the Museum

It seems as if the city's museums are competing to see who can offer the most extracurricular activities. In Washington you don't just visit museums to view art by long-deceased artists; now you can create your own art, see movies, take classes and workshops, attend lectures, and keep your kids busy. The possibilities are endless, from concerts to dance performances to arts and crafts workshops and storytelling. And while many museums are usually closed in the evening, they do offer a host of after-work activities. Some of the ongoing activities are listed in the appropriate chapters in this book, but for a full list of each museum's events, check the events calendar on its Web site.

---

and consists of art from China, Japan, Korea, India, Pakistan, Turkey, Iran, Iraq, and Syria. Along with that of the neighboring Sackler Gallery, the collection forms the National Museum of Asian Art. The Freer also houses a smaller, but no less impressive, collection of American art, including the world's largest collection of Whistler paintings. The gallery also offers a complete schedule of guided tours, performances, Asian films, talks, and activities for children. Open daily except Christmas from 10 a.m. to 5:30 p.m.

Goddard Space Flight Center's Visitor Center
ICESat Road and Greenbelt Road (SR 193)
(301) 286-3978
www.nasa.gov/centers/goddard/visitor

While other museums bring the world to you, the Goddard Visitor Center brings you the universe. See amazing pictures of faraway planets, nebulas, and stars at the Hubble Space Telescope exhibit. Get a peek at NASA's future projects, and stroll through the Rocket Garden to view full-size, retired rockets. Bring the kids along every third Sunday of the month for hands-on activities at The Sunday Experiment. Open Tuesday though Friday from 10 a.m. to 3 p.m. during the spring and fall, 10 a.m. to 5 p.m. in the summer; Saturdays and Sundays, noon to 4 p.m. Closed Sundays during the summer.

Hirshhorn Museum and Sculpture Garden
Independence Avenue and Seventh Street, SW
(202) 633-1000
www.hirshhorn.si.edu

The Hirshhorn Museum and Sculpture Garden houses thousands of works of modern and contemporary art, including artists such as Willem de Kooning, Alexander Calder, Henri Matisse, Francis Bacon, Man Ray, and John Baldessari. Don't know much about modern art? Stop by the information desk for an impromptu thirty-minute tour or ask any of the interpretive guides stationed throughout the galleries. The museum also offers an array of talks, films, tours, and activities for children. Open every day exept Christmas. Museum hours are 10 a.m. to 5:30 p.m., and garden hours are 7:30 a.m. to dusk.

Historical Society of Washington
801 K St., NW (at Mount Vernon Square)
(202) 383-1850
www.historydc.org

While many museums in Washington take a world view on their subjects, the Historical Society of Washington takes a city view. It preserves and promotes the history of the District of Columbia, including its urban landscape and national and international connections. They present rotating exhibits throughout the year, which all have a D.C. focus but often a wider resonance. The society also offers a slew of other free events, including films for adults and children, gardening classes, lectures, concerts, performances, and workshops. Open Tuesday to Sunday, 10 a.m. to 5 p.m.

Historic Blenheim and Civil War Interpretive Center
3610 Old Lee Hwy. (between Old Post Road and Brookwood Drive)
Fairfax, VA
(703) 591-0560
www.fairfaxva.gov/MuseumVC/CivilWarInterpretiveCenter.asp

The Civil War left its mark on Virginia, but nowhere is it more obvious than at Historic Blenheim. Union soldiers occupied the estate and covered its walls with signatures and messages. The Interpretive Center hosts exhibits about the history and meaning of the vintage graffiti, as well as the history of Fairfax during the Civil War. Guided tours are conducted every day at 1 p.m. Open Tuesday to Sunday from noon to 4 p.m.

House of the Temple, Scottish Rite of Freemasonry
1733 16th St., NW (between S Street and Riggs Place)
(202) 232-3579
www.scottishrite.org

Get a glimpse into the mysterious world of the Freemasons at the Grand Lodge, their D.C. headquarters. Walk through the museum to discover the history of the organization, tributes to notable members, and examples of their official regalia. Tours are available throughout the day; Monday to Thursday, 8 a.m. to 5 p.m., and the first Saturday of the month from 10 a.m. to 2 p.m.

Inter-American Development Bank Cultural Center

1300 New York Ave. (between 13th and 14th Streets)
(202) 623-3774
www.iadb.org/cultural

And you thought the only thing creative about banks was their accounting. The Inter-American Development Bank (IDB) assists developing countries in Latin America and the Caribbean and uses its cultural center to help artists in those countries develop a wider audience. The galleries feature established and up-and-coming artists from Latin America and the Caribbean. Guided tours are available upon request. The IDB calendar includes free concerts, films, and lectures. Open Monday to Friday, 11 a.m. to 6 p.m.

The Library of Congress

101 Independence Ave., SE (between 1st Street and South Capitol Street)
(202) 707-5000 (general information)
(202) 707-8000 (visitors' information)
www.loc.gov

The world's largest library has 650 miles of shelves, houses 138 million items in 470 languages, and receives some 22,000 items and adds more than 10,000 of them to its collection every day. The library complex consists of three buildings, but if this is your first visit, start with the Thomas Jefferson Building, at which you can view a rough draft of the Declaration of Independence, the Guttenberg Bible, a map from 1507 that was the first to use the name America, and the breathtaking reading room. Guided tours are offered every day at 10:30 a.m., 11:30 a.m., 1:30 p.m., 2:30 p.m., and 3:30 p.m. The library showcases a number of interactive exhibitions, as well as a full schedule of concerts, lectures, symposia, and readings. Open Monday to Saturday, 8:30 a.m. to 4:30 p.m.

The Lyceum: Alexandria's History Museum

201 South Washington St. (at Prince Street)
Alexandria, VA
(703) 838-4994
oha.alexandriava.gov/lyceum

The Catch $2 suggested donation.

The Lyceum traces the history of Alexandria from its humble beginnings as a Native American fishing village through the Revolutionary and Civil Wars

A Feast for the Eyes
(with an open bar!)

You are cordially invited to rub shoulders with the aristocracy of the D.C. art world. Galleries hold opening receptions for their new shows at which the public can mix and mingle with artists, savor fine wine, and enjoy the chocolate-dipped strawberries. To find out when galleries host receptions, call ahead or join their e-mail mailing lists. Or head to Dupont Circle the first Friday night of the month and enjoy the art and appetizers from all of the area galleries at one time. The First Friday Gallery Walk is a popular D.C. tradition that lures hordes of thirsty art lovers; www.artlineplus.com/gallerymagazine.

Here are some of the galleries that take part in the Dupont Circle First Friday Gallery Walk:

Aaron Gallery, 1717 Connecticut Ave., NW (at R Street); (202) 234-3311; www.aarongallerydc.com

Burton Marinkovich Fine Art, 1506 21st St., NW (between Massachusetts Avenue and P Street); (202) 296-6563; www.burtonmarinkovich.com

Foundry Gallery, 1314 18th St., NW (between Massachusetts Avenue and N Street); (202) 463-0203; www.foundrygallery.org

Gallery 10, Ltd., 1519 Connecticut Ave. NW (at Q Street); (202) 232-3326; www.gallery10dc.com

Hillyer Art Space, 9 Hillyer Court, NW (between 21st Street and Florida Avenue); (202) 338-0680; www.artsandartists.org

to today. The museum also plays host to fun events for children and adults. Open Monday to Saturday, 10 a.m. to 5 p.m.; Sundays, 1 p.m. to 5 p.m.; closed on New Year's Day, Thanksgiving, Christmas Eve, and Christmas.

Mary McLeod Bethune Council House National Historic Site
1318 Vermont Ave., NW (between N Street and Logan Circle)
(202) 673-2402
www.nps.gov/mamc

Marsha Mateyka Gallery, 2012 R St., NW (between 21st Street and Connecticut Avenue); (202) 328-0088; www.marshamateykagallery.com

Studio Gallery, 2108 R St. NW (between 21st Street and Florida Avenue); (202) 232-8734; www.studiogallerydc.com

Other D.C.-Area Galleries of Note:

Addison/Ripley Fine Art, 1670 Wisconsin Ave., NW (at Reservoir Road); (202) 338-5180; www.addisonripleyfineart.com

Discovery Galleries, 4840 Bethesda Ave. (Bethesda Row); Bethesda, MD; (301) 913-9199; www.discoverygalleries.com

The Fraser Gallery, 7700 Wisconsin Ave. (at Middletown Lane), Suite E, Bethesda, MD; (301) 718-9651; www.thefrasergallery.com

Hemphill Fine Arts, 1515 14th St. (at Church Street); (202) 234-5601; www.hemphillfinearts.com

Torpedo Factory Art Center, 105 North Union St. (between King and Cameron Streets); Alexandria, VA; (703) 838-4565; www.torpedofactory.org

Touchstone Gallery, 406 7th St., NW, 2nd Floor (between D and E Streets), (202) 347-2787; www.touchstonegallery.com

Transformer,1404 P St. NW (at 14th St.), (202) 483-1102; www.transformergallery.org

Mary McLeod Bethune was an African-American educator, civil rights leader, and presidential advisor who founded the National Council of Negro Women (NCNW) and Bethune Cookman College. Bethune's final residence, this D.C. townhouse served as the first headquarters for the NCNW and has been restored to capture the feel and style of Bethune's time. Tours are given on a daily basis.

National Academy of Sciences
2101 Constitution Ave., NW (between 20th and 21st Streets)
(202) 334-2436
www.nationalacademies.org/arts

The National Academy of Sciences houses a rotating exhibition of science-centric art and artifacts. Sometimes the science connections are obvious (nature photographs, portraits of important scientists, etc.); other times the science is deconstructed, twisted, and turned inside out. The museum also offers free classical concerts on Sunday afternoons and a full schedule of lectures. Open Monday to Friday, 9 a.m. to 5 p.m.

National Air and Space Museum—National Mall
Independence Avenue at 6th Street, SW
(202) 633-1000
www.nasm.si.edu

Loosen up your neck muscles before you enter the National Air and Space Museum or you're liable to walk out with a stiff neck from looking up at all the eye-popping flying machines on display. As you enter, you're greeted by the Milestones of Flight Gallery, which traces the history of flight from the 1903 Wright Flyer to Charles Lindbergh's *Spirit of St. Louis* to rockets that have taken humans to the moon. The rest of this hangar-size museum is filled with fun, interactive exhibits about flight, including an exhibit designed to answer the most basic question in the most interesting of ways —How We Fly. Guided tours are available every day at 10:30 a.m. and 1 p.m. The museum also offers a full schedule of lectures, children's story times, and other events. Open every day except Christmas from 10 a.m. to 5:30 p.m.

National Air and Space Museum—
Steven F. Udvar-Hazy Center
14390 Air and Space Museum Parkway (near Dulles Airport)
Chantilly, VA
(202) 633-1000
www.nasm.si.edu

The Catch The museum is free, but since it's in the middle of nowhere, you have to pay for parking.

This companion to the National Mall museum is basically its garage, but it's the coolest garage you've ever seen. This huge space is home to thousands of aircraft and artifacts, including engines, helicopters, ultralights, experimental flying machines, historical airplanes, and spacecraft (the Space Shuttle *Enterprise*). Make sure to take a trip to the observation tower to try your hand at being an air traffic controller and get a close-up view of the air traffic at Washington Dulles Airport. Tours are conducted daily at 10:30 a.m. and 1 p.m. Open every day except Christmas from 10 a.m. to 5:30 p.m.

National Archives
700 Constitution Ave., NW (between 7th and 9th Streets)
(866) 272-6272
www.archives.gov

Every important governmental document resides here and can be accessed by anyone. During a visit to the Archives you can see the original Declaration of Independence, Constitution, and Bill of Rights. Meander to the public vaults, where you encounter millions of items, including presidential correspondence, recordings from the Oval Office, historic photos, maps, films, and treaties. Watch the short film about the Archives in the McGowan Theater. The exhibits change throughout the year, and there is also a full schedule of free lectures and documentary films. Open every day except Thanksgiving and Christmas from 10 a.m. to 5:30 p.m.

National Building Museum
401 F St., NW (between 4th and 5th Streets)
(202) 272-2448
www.nbm.org

As you might expect, the building that houses the Building Museum is an architectural achievement of its own. The building's glorious Corinthian columns are among the tallest in the world. The museum's exhibitions run the gamut from the architecture of Washington, D.C., to green building around the world to retrospectives of important architects to origami as architecture. Tours of the building and exhibits are offered on a daily basis. Open Monday to Saturday, 10 a.m. to 5 p.m., and on Sunday from 11 a.m. to 5 p.m.

National Cryptologic Museum
Canine Road and SR 32
Laurel, MD
(301) 688-5849
www.nsa.gov

The NSA is one of the most secretive agencies in the federal government, but the National Cryptologic Museum allows the public to view its code-breaking triumphs. This fascinating museum houses more than 5,000 cryptological artifacts, including everything from the world's oldest cipher to state-of-the-art technology, such as biometrics and microchips. Exhibits explore the unsung heroes and pioneers who put their code-breaking expertise to work during the Civil War, World War II and the Cold War. As you leave the museum, be sure to stop by nearby Vigilance Park for an up-close look at retired fighter jets. The museum is open Monday through Friday from 9 a.m. to 4 p.m.

National Firearms Museum
11250 Waples Mill Rd.
Fairfax, Virginia
(703) 267-1600
www.nationalfirearmsmuseum.org/default.asp

The National Firearms Museum was created by the National Rifle Association and aims to tell you everything wonderful and patriotic about guns in America. Open Monday through Friday 9:30 a.m. to 5 p.m. and until 7 p.m. on Saturday.

National Gallery of Art
4th Street and Constitution Avenue, NW (between 3rd and 9th Streets)
(202) 737-4215
www.nga.gov

The National Gallery of Art is among the top art destinations in the world. With a collection of more than 116,000 works, one can see why. The gallery's collection tracks the development of Western art from the Middle Ages to the present. The classical West Building features European and American art from the 13th to the 19th centuries, such as the only painting by Leonardo da Vinci in the Western Hemisphere, as well as works by Dutch masters and French Impressionists. The modern East Building's collection features major 20th-century artists such as Alexander Calder, Henri Matisse, Joan Miró, Pablo Picasso, Jackson Pollock, and Mark Rothko. Guided tours through the many exhibitions are scheduled throughout the day. The Gallery also offers an impressive number of lectures and symposia, films, and family activities every week. Open every day except Christmas and New Year's Day, Monday through Saturday from 10 a.m. to 5 p.m. and Sunday from 11 a.m. to 6 p.m.

National Gallery of Art Sculpture Garden
4th Street and Constitution Avenue, NW (between 3rd and 9th Streets)
(202) 737-4215
www.nga.gov

This beautifully landscaped six-acre garden is home to a growing collection of modern sculptures, including works by Louise Bourgeois, Roy Lichtenstein, Sol LeWitt, and David Smith, among others. Tours are conducted from August 1 to October 31, weather permitting, on Fridays at 12:30 p.m. and Saturdays at 1:30 p.m. Open Memorial Day through Labor Day, Monday to Thursday and Saturday, 10 a.m. to 7 p.m.; Friday, 10 a.m. to 9:30 p.m.; and Sunday, 11 a.m. to 7:00 p.m.

National Geographic Museum
1145 17th St., NW (at M Street)
(202) 857-7588
www.ngmuseum.org

National Geographic's expeditions, adventures, and scientific research leap from the pages of the magazine to the halls of its museum. The ever-changing exhibitions explore the existence of wildlife around the world, distant cultures, ancient traditions, and today's scientific revelations and introduce you to the people who bring these stories and startling images to life. Open every day except Christmas, Monday to Saturday, 9 a.m. to 5 p.m., and Sundays, 10 a.m. to 5 p.m. Check out the free film series every Tuesday at noon.

National Guard Memorial Museum
One Massachusetts Ave., NW (at North Capital Street)
(888) 226-4287
www.ngef.org

"National Guardsmen are: citizens most of the time, soldiers some of the time, patriots all of the time." This quote at the entryway sets the tone for this museum, which traces the history of the National Guard. Using movies, interactive displays, uniforms, and artifacts, the museum examines the Guard's beginnings in 1636 to the vital role it plays in the post–September 11 military. Open 10 a.m. to 4 p.m., Monday through Friday.

National Museum of African Art

950 Independence Ave., SW (between 7th and 14th Street)
(202) 633-4600
http://africa.si.edu

The National Museum of African Art showcases diverse art from the Dark Continent, from ancient objects to contemporary paintings, sculptures, and printmaking. The museum is part of the Smithsonian Institution, so it offers plenty of free activities, including tours, film, discussions, lectures, and lively performances. Open every day except Christmas from 10 a.m. to 5:30 p.m.

National Museum of American History

14th Street and Constitution Avenue, NW
(202) 633-1000
www.americanhistory.si.edu

The National Museum of American History effectively showcases every object and symbol of social, cultural, and political importance in the country. Highlights include the top hat Abraham Lincoln wore the night of his assassination; Dorothy's ruby slippers from *The Wizard of Oz*; a 40-foot stretch of the famed US Route 66; a five-story-tall, 23-room dollhouse; the inaugural gowns of fourteen First Ladies; Julia Child's kitchen; a backyard bomb shel-

Gotcha!

Although you won't have to open your wallet to get into any of these museums, be warned you may have to dig deep once you're inside their hallowed halls. Most museums offer no shortage of cafes, restaurants, and snack bars. Lunch for a family of four usually runs anywhere from $50 to $100, depending on the restaurant. If you are making a day of it, definitely pack your lunch and take along your water bottle. Another area in which you'll have to shell out serious cash is parking. For any museums within the District, you'll be hardpressed to find any free parking, and if you do, it's usually limited to an hour or two. The Metro, though no bargain either, is still your best option for getting around D.C. The good news is that most of the destinations outside the city do offer free parking. Check their Web sites for details.

ter; the actual flag that inspired "The Star-Spangled Banner;" a Georgian-style, two-and-a-half-story timber-framed house (the largest artifact in the museum); the original Kermit the Frog and Miles Davis's trumpet. Guided tours run every day at 10 a.m. and 1 p.m. Open every day except Christmas from 10 a.m. to 5:30 p.m.

National Museum of American Jewish Military History
1811 R St., NW (between 18th and 19th Streets)
(202) 265-6280
www.nmajmh.org

This museum was created by the Jewish War Veterans of the USA with the aim of documenting and recognizing the heroism and sacrifice of Jewish-Americans in the armed forces. Open Monday to Friday, 9 a.m. to 5 p.m.

National Museum of Health and Medicine
Walter Reed Army Medical Center
6900 Georgia Ave., NW (at Elder Street)
Building 54
(202) 782-2200
www.nmhm.washingtondc.museum

Not since that fateful night at Ford's Theatre have Abraham Lincoln and John Wilkes Booth been in the same place. But at the National Museum of Health and Medicine, some of their remains are on display. In this fascinating museum of medical wonders, curiosities, oddities, and forensic feats, you can view Lincoln's blood-stained shirt, his skull fragments, and the bullet that killed him, and a section of Booth's spine where he was shot and killed. Other exhibits at the museum include "Human Body, Human Being" which features preserved human specimens, giving visitors the pleasure of comparing a smoker's lung to a coal miner's lung, of touching the inside of a stomach and of viewing skeletons, skulls, and a brain still attached to a spinal cord suspended in formaldehyde. "From a Single Cell" documents the detailed development of a person from an embryo to five years of age. You can grab a Listening Wand and take a self-guided tour around the museum or check its schedule for tours. Take the budding CSI in your family to the museum's "Family Forensics Discovery" activities on Saturday afternoons. Open every day except Christmas from 10 a.m. to 5:30 p.m.

National Museum of Natural History
1000 Constitution Ave. (between 9th and 12th Streets, NW)
(202) 633-1000
www.mnh.si.edu

What do you get when you put together thirty million insects, four-and-a-half million plants, seven million fish, a hall full of dinosaurs, and an African elephant? You get one of the pre-eminent natural history museums in the world, with live presentations, specimens, interactive exhibits, artifacts, recreations, old bones, and new technology. Under one roof, visitors can find every scientific subject from anthropology to zoology. No trip is complete without spending time in the Dinosaur Hall, the Sant Ocean Hall, and the Hall of Bones and viewing the cursed Hope Diamond. The Butterfly Hall is mesmerizing, but make sure you plan to visit on Tuesday, when it's free. Stop by the Butterfly box office for free timed entrance tickets. Kids will be happily grossed out in the Orkin Insect Zoo (tarantula feedings daily). Keep yourself busy with a plethora of lectures, performances, films, and children's activities. Guided tours are available throughout the day. Open every day except Christmas from 10 a.m. to 5:30 p.m.

National Museum of the American Indian
Fourth Street and Independence Ave., SW
(202) 633-1000
www.nmai.si.edu

With its authentic landscaping and design, visitors to the National Museum of the American Indian are immediately transported to a Native American reservation. The museum is overflowing with dazzling artifacts, interactive displays, firsthand oral histories, music, and crafts. The changing exhibits explore the histories, beliefs, customs, art, and cultures of these once-vast civilizations. The museum also offers a full schedule of lectures, films, and children's activities. Tours are conducted at 1:30 p.m. and 3 p.m. every day with an additional tour at 11 a.m. on the weekends. Open every day except Christmas from 10 a.m. to 5:30 p.m.

National Museum of the Marine Corps
18900 Jefferson Davis Hwy. (near Quantico Marine Base)
Triangle, VA
(877) 635-1775
www.usmcmuseum.com

The Catch Some exhibits are graphic and are not appropriate for young children.

From the outside you're struck by the dramatic spire of the museum, which is reminiscent of the iconic image of the raising of the flag at Iwo Jima. Once you step inside the National Museum of the Marine Corps, you're drawn into its stories of Marines throughout the Corps' more-than-230-year history. Through interactive exhibits, artifacts, films, and hands-on activities, the museum gives visitors a chance to experience life as a Marine, including realistic recreations of battlefields during World War II, Korea, and Vietnam. Some of the exhibits are graphic and may not be appropriate for young children. Guided tours take place at 10 a.m., noon, and 2 p.m. every day. Open every day except Christmas from 9 a.m. to 5 p.m.

National Portrait Gallery
8th and F Streets, NW
(202) 633-8300
www.npg.si.edu

See the story of America through the portraits of the people who shaped its history, development, and culture. The National Portrait Gallery's collection begins with its series of official presidential portraits and expands to include portraits from the art, sports, science, history, and political worlds. The museum's vast compilation runs from 1600 to today and includes everyone from Elizabeth I to Elizabeth Taylor. Guided tours are conducted weekdays at 11:45 a.m. and 2:15 p.m. and weekends at 11:45 a.m. and 3:15 p.m. Open every day from 11:30 a.m. to 7 p.m.

National Postal Museum
2 Massachusetts Ave., NE (between North Capital and 1st Streets)
(202) 633-5555
www.postalmuseum.si.edu

Located in a majestic building that served as the D.C. post office from 1914 to 1986, the National Postal Museum tracks the development of the postal service with displays of vintage airplanes, coaches, and railroad cars. Starting with Ben Franklin, the first Postmaster General, one sees the progression of transporting the mail, from stagecoaches to the Pony Express to building the railroads to airmail. The museum is also home to the world's largest collection of stamps. Call the museum to find out when tours are available.

Navy Memorial and Naval Heritage Center
701 Pennsylvania Ave., NW, Suite 123 (between 7th and 9th Streets)
(202) 737-2300
www.navymemorial.org

While the Navy Museum focuses on naval history, battles, and artifacts, the Navy Memorial and Naval Heritage Center puts the spotlight on naval veterans. The plaza is a tribute to The Lone Sailor, an emotional memorial to sailors past and present. The Heritage Center offers changing exhibitions on specific areas of the navy, such as the medical corps and the Blue Angels. Open every day except Thanksgiving, Christmas, and New Year's Day from 9:30 a.m. to 5 p.m.

Navy Museum
Washington Navy Yard
805 Kidder Breeze St., SE (enter Navy Yard at O Street)
(202) 433-4882
www.history.navy.mil/branches/org8-9.htm

The Navy Museum takes you through the history of the navy, from the Revolutionary War to today, with lots of opportunities to see and touch objects, including ships large and small, deep-sea diving uniforms, ship guns, submarines, and vintage uniforms. After exploring the museum, take a tour of the USS *Barry*, which is parked across from the museum. Because of increased security, it is a good idea to call before you visit. Open Monday to Friday from 9 a.m. to 5 p.m. and on the weekends from 10 a.m. to 5 p.m.

Old Stone House
3051 M St., NW (between 30th and 31st Streets)
(202) 426-6851
www.nps.gov/olst

Built in 1765, the Old Stone House is the oldest surviving structure in Washington, D.C. This colonial-era home is preserved with period artifacts and furnishings. A walk though the house won't take you more than ten minutes, but it's a perfect way to escape the Georgetown crowds. Open Wednesday through Sunday, noon to 5 p.m.

The Phillips Collection
1600 21st St., NW (at Q Street)
(202) 387-2151
www.phillipscollection.org

The Catch Free Tuesday through Friday, with a suggested donation.

Once the home of the collection's namesake, The Phillips Collection was the first modern art museum in the United States. Although the home has expanded, it remains an intimate space for viewing an extensive collection of Impressionist and modern artists such as Renoir and Rothko, Bonnard and O'Keeffe, Van Gogh, and Diebenkorn. A short spotlight tour is conducted every weekday at noon. Gallery talks are scheduled every Thursday evening, and don't miss "Phillips after 5," a lecture and entertainment extravaganza on the first Thursday of every month. Open Tuesday to Saturday from 10 a.m. to 5 p.m. (Thursdays until 8:30 p.m.) and Sundays from 11 a.m. to 6 p.m. The museum is free with a suggested donation on weekdays only.

Radio & Television Museum of Bowie
2608 Mitchellville Rd. (at Mt. Oak Road)
Bowie, MD
(301) 390-1020
www.radiohistory.org

Explore the Radio & Television Museum of Bowie's hands-on exhibits and extensive collection of vintage radios and TVs, from Marconi's earliest wireless telegraph to the primitive crystal TV sets of the 1920s. Open Tuesday to Sunday, noon to 4 p.m.

Renwick Gallery
1661 Pennsylvania Ave., NW (at 17th Street)
(202) 633-1000
www.americanart.si.edu

Located just steps from the White House, the Renwick Gallery is the Smithsonian American Art Museum's home for American crafts and contemporary decorative arts from the 1800s on. The permanent collection consists of vintage furniture and jewelry created from clay, fiber, glass, metal, wood, or any combination of those. Tours of the collection are held weekdays at noon and at 1 p.m. on the weekends. Open every day except Christmas from 10 a.m. to 5:30 p.m.

Reston Museum
1639 Washington Plaza (Lake Anne Village Center)
Reston, VA
(703) 709-7700
www.restonmuseum.org

Located in historic Lake Anne Village, the Reston Museum traces the history of Reston from its establishment in 1961, when Robert E. Simon acquired the land, to today. Exhibits include the original 8' by 11' master plan model of the town, oral histories, and artifacts. The museum hosts walking tours, concerts, and a very popular children's art class on Saturday mornings. Open Tuesday to Friday and Sunday from noon to 5 p.m. and on Saturday from 10 a.m. to 5 p.m.

Sackler Gallery
1050 Independence Ave., SW (between 9th and 12th Streets)
(202) 633-1000
www.asia.si.edu

Along with the neighboring Freer Gallery, the collection forms the National Museum of Asian Art. Building on the permanent collection at the Freer, the Sackler features Asian art, including Persian literature from the 11th century to the 19th century; 19th- and 20th-century Japanese prints and contemporary porcelain; Indian, Chinese, Japanese, Korean, and South Asian paintings; and Japanese sculpture and ceramics. A variety of guided tours is given every day at the museum. Open every day except Christmas from 10 a.m. to 5:30 p.m.

Sewall-Belmont House and Museum
144 Constitution Ave., NE
(202) 546-1210
www.sewallbelmont.org

The Catch $5 suggested donation

The Sewall-Belmont House and Museum is the home of the women's rights movement in the United States. Alice Paul, a leading suffragist, once lived here. Paul was jailed for leading the first protest at the White House for women's suffrage and is the author of the Equal Rights Amendment and the founder of the National Women's Party. The home was the headquarters of the National Women's Party and now serves as a suffragist museum. Take a tour of historic items such as Susan B. Anthony's desk; Elizabeth Cady Stanton's chair; original suffrage banners used in picketing and parades; photos; cartoons; and more. Tours are available on the hour, Wednesdays through Sundays from noon to 3 p.m. There is a suggested donation of $5.

Smithsonian American Art Museum
8th and F Streets NW
(202) 633-1000
www.americanart.si.edu

The Smithsonian American Art Museum shares a palatial building with the National Portrait Gallery and is home to 300 years of American art. Its walls are full of landmark works by artists such as Winslow Homer, John Singer, Georgia O'Keeffe, Edward Hopper, Jacob Lawrence, Christo, David Hockney, and Robert Rauschenberg. The museum's collections include New Deal art, American Impressionist paintings, masterpieces from the Gilded Age, folk art, work by African-American and Latino artists, and photography. The museum's schedule of activities, events, and performances include drawing workshops, gallery talks (with free coffee or tea), scavenger hunts, opera, jazz, and classical concerts. Highlight tours are offered daily at 12:30 p.m. and 2 p.m. Open every day except Christmas from 11:30 a.m. to 7 p.m.

Smithsonian Castle
1100 Jefferson Dr., SW (between 7th and 14th Streets)
(202) 633-1000
www.si.edu/visit/whatsnew/sib.asp

The Smithsonian Castle is more formally known as the Smithsonian Information Center and serves as the starting point for a visit to the Smithsonian's seventeen D.C. museums and the National Zoo. Get answers to all of your Smithsonian questions, gather Smithsonian maps and brochures, and watch an introductory Smithsonian video. Check out "America's Treasure Chest," an informative exhibit about the organization's magnificent collection that's spread across the museums. There are also changing exhibits in the Castle's other galleries, as well as beautiful gardens. Open every day except Christmas from 9 a.m. to 5 p.m.

Smithsonian International Gallery
Ripley Center
1100 Jefferson Dr., SW (between the Castle and Freer Gallery)
(202) 633-1000
www.si.edu/ripley/ig

The Smithsonian International Gallery offers a selection of pricey limited-edition prints and posters commissioned by the Smithsonian. The gallery also presents changing exhibitions throughout the year, including many of the Smithsonian's traveling shows and overflow exhibitions from the other D.C.-based museums. Open every day except Christmas from 10 a.m. to 5:30 p.m.

Textile Museum
2320 S St., NW (between 23rd and 24th Streets)
(202) 667-0441
www.textilemuseum.org

The Catch Admission is free, but there is a suggested donation.

The Textile Museum's collection of foreign rugs and textiles includes more than 18,000 pieces that span 5,000 years, dating from 3,000 B.C. to the present. Exhibitions include a huge collection of Oriental rugs and early-Islamic and pre-Columbian Peruvian textiles. Take a moment to relax in the lovely garden, with its beautiful view of the city. The museum offers textile-appreciation lectures every Saturday at 10:30 a.m. and family activities on the first Saturday of the month, as well as many other talks and tours. Tour the museum every Saturday and Sunday at 1 p.m. Open Tuesday through Saturday, 10 a.m. to 5 p.m., and Sunday 1 to 5 p.m.

United States Holocaust Memorial Museum
100 Raoul Wallenberg Place SW (between Independence and Main Avenues)
(202) 488-0400
www.ushmm.org

The Catch Free tickets are required March through August. You will have to pay a $1.75 service charge to get advance tickets online.

The United States Holocaust Memorial Museum serves as a monument to the more than six million victims of Nazi genocide. The museum presents a narrative history of the Holocaust with its more than 90,000 artifacts and historic photos, seventy video monitors, and four theaters. Exhibitions appear on three floors and are divided into three parts: "Nazi Assault," "Final Solution," and "Last Chapter." Some of the especially moving displays include a railcar that took victims to concentration camps, a three-story tower of pictures of the residents of a Latvian town who were massacred over the course of two days and many oral histories and eyewitness testimonies from survivors. Plan to spend two to three hours for the self-guided tour of the exhibition. From March through August visitors need to obtain a free, timed entry pass to view the permanent exhibit. The museum distributes a limited number of tickets for same-day use every day starting at 10 a.m., or you can get advance tickets through its Web site. From September to February no entry passes are needed. A number of temporary exhibits don't require a pass. Open every day from 10 a.m. to 5:30 p.m. except on Yom Kippur and Christmas Day.

United States Patent and Trademarks Office Museum
The Madison Building
600 Dulany St. (between Emerson and Eisenhower Avenues)
Alexandria, VA
(571) 272-0095
www.uspto.gov/web/offices/ac/ahrpa/opa/museum/

The United States Patent and Trademarks Museum brings the history of American invention to life. The portrait gallery features six portraits of important patent holders, including Thomas Jefferson, Thomas Edison, and Steve Wozniak (cofounder of Apple Computer). Each portrait spontaneously becomes animated and interacts with the others, telling viewers a story about America's intellectual property system. It may sound boring, but the museum presents it in an inventive way. Walk through the Inventors Hall of Fame and rotating exhibitions to learn how specific inventions and inventors have shaped our country and the world. Open Monday to Friday, 9 a.m. to 5 p.m., and Saturday from noon to 5 p.m.

Waters House History Center
12535 Milestone Manor Lane (Waters House Park)
Germantown, MD
(301) 515-2887
www.montgomeryhistory.org

Walk through this historic home that dates back to the 1790s. The Waters House History Center is run by the Montgomery County Historical Society, which also uses the space as a gallery for rotating exhibits about the history of Montgomery County. Open Wednesdays and Saturdays from 10 a.m. to 4 p.m.

Women in Military Service for America Memorial
Arlington National Cemetery
Memorial Bridge and Jefferson Davis Highway
(703) 533-1155
www.womensmemorial.org

The exhibitions at the Women in Military Service for America Memorial recount and commemorate the often-forgotten role women have played, and continue to play, in the military in every conflict since the Revolutionary War. Call in advance to arrange tours. Open every day except Christmas from 8 a.m. to 5 p.m. from October through March and till 7 p.m. from April through September.

ROMANCE: **SWEET NOTHINGS**

"If you want to say it with flowers,
a single rose says: 'I'm cheap!'"

—DELTA BURKE

Hey, even cheap bastards need love. And while it may be true that introducing yourself by saying, "Hi, I'm a cheap bastard" might not be the most successful way to get a date, being a cheap bastard shouldn't get in the way of having a great time. You might even score extra points by coming up with original ideas for romantic liaisons around D.C. Here's a list of great ways to spend days and evenings with that special someone that won't cost you a thing (except maybe your heart).

The Untraditional Traditional Date: Why not put a twist on the usual date by seeing a free movie. During the summer, lay out a blanket and cuddle with your baby as you enjoy a starlit night and a Hollywood movie. Favorite summer festivals include "River Front Reels" and "Crystal Screen or Movies on the Lawn." During the cooler months, move indoors with the free screenings at the National Gallery or Library of Congress or make it dinner and a movie at American City Diner or EatBar. For more details and other film destinations, see pages 45–58.

The Sweep-Her-Off-Her-Feet Date: Make the night a little spicy with free salsa lessons and dancing every Monday night at Lima restaurant. To make it a little more Cheap Bastard–friendly, ladies drink free from 9 p.m. until 11 p.m. Think you're ready to make more of a commitment? Take the free six-week tango class at the Embassy of Argentina. For details and more dance ideas, see pages 64–69.

The Let's-Get-Sweaty Date: Hop on a bike and ride down the C & O Canal towpath or join in on a guided tour through the park. Any relationship calls for a little flexibility, and you can show yours off at free yoga classes at

Lululemon or Boundless Yoga. And if things are getting a bit tense between the two of you, free kung fu classes at the Chinese Cultural Community Center might be in order to work off some of that tension. For more fitness ideas see pages 151–165.

The Music-Is-the-Food-of-Love Date: All right, you may not have the voice to serenade your sweetheart, but plenty of talented local musicians can set the mood for you. Whatever kind of music strikes a chord with your date, you can find it: reggae at Chief Ike's Mambo Room, jazz at the Smithsonian American Art Museum, classical at the National Gallery of Art, and everything in between at the Kennedy Center's Millennium Stage. For other music listings see pages 25–43.

The Au Naturel Date: Tag along for a birdwatching tour with the Audubon Society or a moonlight hike through the National Arboretum. For more naturalist tours see pages 182–188; for gardens see pages 196–200.

The Pretentious Date: Show your date you know the difference between Cubist, Conceptualist, Minimalist, and Post-Modernist with a visit to the Dupont Circle First Friday Gallery Walk or other weekly gallery openings. For more about art museums, see pages 202–228.

The Show'em-You-Got-Class Date: Take in a museum. Most museums have free admission. Not only are D.C.'s museums filled with priceless art and world-class collections, many offer independent films, and documentaries; classical, jazz, and world music concerts and classes; and lectures by intellectuals from around the world. See the museum listings on pages 201–228.

The Not-Quite-the-Great-White-Way Date: Take my advice: if you want a second date, don't try this on a first date. If you've been dating for a while, and it is clear that you're both Cheap Bastards, then why not pick out a show at any of D.C.'s major theaters and volunteer to usher together? If you don't want to seem quite that cheap, most theaters offer pay-what-you-can performances during the run of every show. See the theater listings on pages 3–22.

The Power-Is-the-Ultimate-Aphrodisiac Date: They say politics makes strange bedfellows, so why not walk the halls of power at the Capitol, take in oral arguments at the Supreme Court, or take a shot at making your own scandal during a visit to the White House. For details and more tours, see pages 175–182.

The Hey-This-Is-Going-Pretty-Swell, I-May-Just-Want-to-Kiss-You Special Add-On to Any Date: If you want to end your date on a high note, plant one with the dramatic D.C. skyline as a backdrop from atop the Kennedy Center (page 177) or the Old Post Office tower (page 177).

FINDING A **CHEAP** DATE

Ehh, I mean finding a date, cheaply. It's a big city with lots of single people, but hanging out in bars and going to "singles" parties and events can be costly, not to mention depressing. Here are a couple of alternative ways to make the connection by volunteering and just being your own cheap self.

Professionals in the City
(202) 686-5990
www.prosinthecity.com

The Catch Volunteer for free admission.

Professionals in the City hosts singles events almost every night of the week, from four-minute dating to mixers, classes, holiday parties, and weekend trips. You can volunteer to join some but not all events. Two of their most popular events every year are the singles Passover Seder and New Year's Eve party, during which they need a lot of help. Hundreds of singles attend these events at $50 to $200 a pop, but you can slip in for free by lending a hand; just show up an hour early to help set up and then enjoy yourself. You can also get out of town for free on one of their weekend trips if you do the driving. Contact them a month or so in advance to sign up to staff a party or make arrangements for a weekend trip. They do not take volunteers for the four-minute dating events, but check their schedule for other large events throughout the year.

Single Volunteers of D.C.
www.svdc.org

It is really a very simple but ingenious concept: bring socially minded single people together to help others, and love may flourish. Anyone can join the group for free through its Web site and then sign up for volunteer opportunities. You may find yourself preparing meals for people battling HIV/AIDS or cancer, pulling weeds in a nature sanctuary, marching in the 4th of July parade, answering phones for a telethon or building a house for Habitat for Humanity. SVDC works with non- and not-for-profit groups throughout the area to find engaging and positive activities for groups of volunteers (usually with even numbers of men and women). Some events are for specific age groups, but all are open to gay, lesbian, and straight singles.

APPENDIX B:

PUBLIC LIBRARIES: **FREE ACCESS**

"No entertainment is so cheap as reading,
nor any pleasure so lasting."
—LADY MARY WORTLEY MONTAGU

Libraries are the ultimate resource for anyone who wants it all but doesn't want to spend anything to get it. Of course, D.C. is home to the mother of all libraries, the Library of Congress. And while the LOC has it all, it doesn't lend out its books, and the general public doesn't usually make use of its voluminous stacks. For more about the LOC, see page 35.

For day-to-day use, Washington's public libraries serve the public the best. At each of the seventy-eight branches in the area, patrons can scour shelves of books, DVDs, and CDs. Forget about that Netflix subscription, the libraries have it: Hollywood hits, documentaries, TV shows, and service DVDs. There is even a large collection of audiobooks, e-books and test-prep software that you can download from home for free. The branches all have computers for public use and free access to the Internet (many with Wi-Fi), as well as computer classes.You can also find free classes in everything from qigong and knitting to job-hunting skills and starting a small business. Almost every public library has story times and activities for children and a regular schedule of music, films, theater, and readings. Check the Web sites or stop into any branch to get schedules of classes and activities.

D.C. Public Libraries

Martin Luther King Jr., 901 G St., NW; (202) 727-0321
Anacostia Interim, 1800 Good Hope Rd., SE; (202) 715-7707/7708
Benning Interim, 4101 Benning Rd., NE; (202) 442-7740/7741
Capitol View, 5001 Central Ave., SE; (202) 645-0755
Chevy Chase, 5625 Connecticut Ave., NW; (202) 282-0021
Cleveland Park, 3310 Connecticut Ave., NW; (202) 282-3080
Francis A. Gregory, 3660 Alabama Ave., SE; (202) 645-4297
Georgetown Interim, 3307 M St., NW; (202) 724-8783

Juanita E. Thornton/Shepherd Park, 7420 Georgia Ave., NW; (202) 541-6100

Lamond-Riggs, 5401 South Dakota Ave., NE; (202) 541-6255

Mount Pleasant, 3160 16th St., NW; (202) 671-0200

Northeast, 330 7th St., NE; (202) 698-3320

Palisades, 4901 V St., NW; (202) 282-3139

Parklands-Turner, 1700 Alabama Ave., SE; (202) 698-1103

Petworth, 4200 Kansas Ave., NW; (202) 541-6300

R. L. Christian, 1300 H St., NE; (202) 724-8599

Southeast, 403 7th St., SE; (202) 698-3377

Southwest, 900 Wesley Place, SW; (202) 724-4752

Takoma Park, 416 Cedar St., NW; (202) 576-7252

Tenley-Friendship Interim, 4200 Wisconsin Ave., NW; (202) 244-3212

Washington Highlands, 115 Atlantic St., SW; (202) 645-5880

Watha T. Daniel/Shaw Interim, 945 Rhode Island Ave., NW; (202) 671-0265/0267

West End, 1101 24th St., NW; (202) 724-8707

Woodridge, 801 Hamlin St., NE; (202) 541-6226

www.dclibrary.org

Montgomery County (MD) Public Libraries

Aspen Hill, 4407 Aspen Hill Rd., Rockville, MD; (240) 773-9410

Bethesda, 7400 Arlington Rd., Bethesda, MD; (240) 777-0970

Chevy Chase, 8005 Connecticut Ave., Chevy Chase, MD; (240) 773-9590

Damascus, 9701 Main St., Damascus, MD; (240) 773-9444

Davis, 6400 Democracy Blvd., Bethesda, MD; (240) 777-0922

Gaithersburg, 18330 Montgomery Village Ave., Gaithersburg, MD; (240) 773-9490

Germantown, 19840 Century Blvd., Germantown, MD; (240) 777-0110

Kensington Park, 4201 Knowles Ave., Kensington, MD; (240) 773-9515

Little Falls, 5501 Massachusetts Ave., Bethesda, MD; (240) 773-9520

Long Branch, 8800 Garland Ave., Silver Spring, MD; (240) 777-0910

Marilyn J. Praisner Fairland, 14910 Old Columbia Pike, Burtonsville, MD; (240) 773-9460

Noyes Library for Young Children, 10237 Carroll Place, Kensington, MD; (240) 773-9570

Olney, 3500 Olney-Laytonsville Rd., Olney, MD; (240) 773-9545

Poolesville, 19633 Fisher Ave., Poolesville, MD; (240) 773-9550
Potomac, 10101 Glenolden Dr., Potomac, MD; (240) 777-0690
Quince Orchard, 15831 Quince Orchard Rd., Gaithersburg, MD; (240) 777-0200
Rockville, 21 Maryland Ave., Rockville, MD; (240) 777-0140
Silver Spring, 8901 Colesville Rd., Silver Spring, MD; (240) 773-9420
Twinbrook, 202 Meadow Hall Dr., Rockville, MD; (240) 777-0240
Wheaton, 11701 Georgia Ave., Wheaton, MD; (240) 777-0678
White Oak, 11701 New Hampshire Ave., Silver Spring, MD; (240) 773-9555
www.montgomerycountymd.gov/libraries

Prince George's County (MD) Memorial Library System
Accokeek, 15773 Livingston Rd.; Accokeek, MD; (301) 292-2880
Baden, 13603 Baden-Westwood Rd., Brandywine, MD; (301) 888-1152
Beltsville, 4319 Sellman Rd., Beltsville, MD; (301) 937-0294
Bladensburg, 4820 Annapolis Rd., Bladensburg, MD; (301) 927-4916
Bowie, 15210 Annapolis Rd., Bowie, MD; (301) 262-7000
Fairmont Heights, 5904 Kolb St., Fairmount Heights, MD; (301) 883-2650
Glenarden, 8724 Glenarden Parkway, Glenarden, MD; (301) 772-5477
Greenbelt, 11 Crescent Rd., Greenbelt, MD; (301) 345-5800
Hillcrest Heights, 2398 Iverson St., Temple Hills, MD; (301) 630-4900
Hyattsville, 6530 Adelphi Rd., Hyattsville, MD; (301) 985-4690
Largo, 9601 Capital Lane, Largo, MD; (301) 336-4044
Laurel, 507 7th St., Laurel, MD; (301) 776-6790
Upper Marlboro, 14730 Main St., Upper Marlboro, MD; (301) 627-9330
Mount Rainier, 3409 Rhode Island Ave., Mount Rainier, MD; (301) 864-8937
New Carrollton, 7414 Riverdale Rd., New Carrollton, MD; (301) 459-6900
Oxon Hill, 6200 Oxon Hill Rd., Oxon Hill, MD; (301) 839-2400
Spauldings, 5811 Old Silver Hill Rd., District Heights, MD; (301) 817-3750
Surratts-Clinton, 9400 Piscataway Rd., Clinton, MD; (301) 868-9200
www.prge.lib.md.us

Alexandria (VA) Library
Charles E. Beatley, Jr. Central Library, 5005 Duke St., Alexandria, VA; (703) 519-5900
Kate Waller Barrett Branch, 717 Queen St., Alexandria, VA; (703) 838-4555

Ellen Coolidge Burke Branch, 4701 Seminary Rd., Alexandria, VA; (703) 519-6000

James M. Duncan Branch Library, 2501 Commonwealth Ave., Alexandria, VA; (703) 838-4566

Local History/Special Collections, 717 Queen St., Alexandria, VA; (703) 838-4577

www.alexandria.lib.va.us

Arlington (VA) Public Library

Central Library, 1015 North Quincy St., Arlington, VA; (703) 228-5990

Cherrydale Library, 2190 North Military Rd., Arlington, VA; (703) 228-6330

Columbia Pike Library, 816 South Walter Reed Dr., Arlington, VA; (703) 228-5710

Glencarlyn Library, 300 South Kensington St., Arlington, VA; (703) 228-6548

Plaza Library, 2100 Clarendon Blvd., 1st floor lobby, Arlington, VA; (703) 228-3352

Shirlington Library, 4200 Campbell Ave., Arlington, VA; (703) 228-6545

Westover Library, 1800 North Lexington St., Arlington, VA; (703) 228-5260

www.arlingtonva.us

APPENDIX C:

MUNICIPAL RECREATION CENTERS
& POOLS

Washington, D.C., Fitness Centers

Fitness Center: $125 for residents/$150 for non-residents
Pools: free for residents/$130 for non-residents

Ward 1
Columbia Heights Community Center, 1480 Girard St., NW (between 14th and 15th Streets); (202) 671-0373

Ward 2
Kennedy Recreation Center, 1401 7th St., NW (between P and O Streets); (202) 671-4794

Ward 3
Palisades Community Center, 5200 Sherrier Place, NW; (202) 282-2186

Ward 4
Emery Recreation Center, 5801 Georgia Ave., NW (between Madison Street and Missouri Avenue); (202) 576-3211

Lamond Recreation Center, 20 Tuckerman St., NE (at N Capitol Street); (202) 576-9541

Riggs LaSalle Community Center, 501 Riggs Rd., NE (between Madison and Nicholson Streets); (202) 576-5224

Takoma Community Center, 300 Van Buren St., NW (at 3rd Street); (202) 576-7068

Ward 5
North Michigan Park Recreation Center, 1333 Emerson St., NE (between 13th and 14th Streets); (202) 541-3526

Ward 6
King Greenleaf Recreation Center, 201 N St., SW (at Canal Street); (202) 645-7454

Sherwood Recreation Center, 640 10th St., NE (between F and G Streets); (202) 698-3075

Ward 7

Hillcrest Recreation Center, 3100 Denver St., SE (at 32nd Street); (202) 645-9200

www.hillcrestdc.com/reccenter.htm

Ward 8

Anacostia Fitness Center, 1800 Anacostia Dr., SE (at South Capitol Street); (202) 698-2250

Bald Eagle Recreation Center, 100 Joliet St., SW (at 1st Street); (202) 645-3960

Washington, D.C., Indoor Pools

Ward 1

Marie Reed Recreation Center, 2200 Champlain St., NW (at 18th and California Avenue); (202) 673-7768

Ward 4

Takoma Community Center, 300 Van Buren St., NW (between 3rd and 5th Streets); (202) 576-7068

Ward 5

Dunbar Aquatic Facility, 1301 New Jersey Ave., NW (at N Street); (202) 673-4316

Turkey Thicket Recreation Center, 1100 Michigan Ave., NE (between Perry and 10th Street); (202) 576-9238

Thurgood Marshall Recreation Center, 3100 Fort Lincoln Dr., NE (at 33rd Place); (202) 576-6818

Ward 6

Rumsey Aquatic Center, 635 North Carolina Ave., SE (between 6th and 7th Streets); (202) 724-4495

Ward 7

D.C. Center for Therapeutic Recreation, 3030 G St., SE (between 31st Street and Bayley Place); (202) 698-1794

Ward 8

Ferebee Hope Recreation Center, 3999 8th St., SE (at Yuma Street); (202) 645-3917

Washington, D.C., Outdoor Pools

Ward 1

Banneker Community Center, 2500 Georgia Ave., NW (between Howard Place and Euclid Street); (202) 673-6861

Parkview Community Center, 693 Otis Place, NW (between Warder and 6th Streets); (202) 576-5750

Ward 2

East Potomac Pool, 972 Ohio Dr., SW (East Potomac Park); (202) 727-6523

Francis Pool, 25th and N Streets, NW; (202) 727-3285

Upshur Recreation Center, 4300 Arkansas Ave., NW (at Vamum Street); (202) 576-6842

Volta Park Recreation Center (formerly Georgetown), 1555 34th St., NW (between Q and Volta Streets); (202) 282-0380

Ward 5

Harry Thomas, Sr. Community Center, 1743 Lincoln Rd., NE (between Randolph Place and S Street); (202) 576-5642

Langdon Park Community Center, 2901 20th St., NE (between Franklin and Hamlin Streets); (202) 576-6595

Theodore Hagans, Jr. Pool, 3201 Fort Lincoln Dr., NE (between 31st Street and 33rd Place); (202) 576-6389

Ward 6

Rosedale Recreation Center, 1701 Gales St., NE (at 17th Street); (202) 724-5405

Randall Pool, South Capitol and I Streets, SW; (202) 727-1420

Ward 7

Benning Park, Southern Avenue and Fable Street, SE; (202) 645-5044

Fort Dupont Pool, Ridge Road and Burns Street, SE; (202) 645-5046

Kelly Miller Recreation Center, 301 49th St., NE (between Clay and Dix Streets); (202) 388-6895

Kenilworth-Parkside Recreation Center, 4300 Anacostia Ave., NE (at Nash Street); (202) 727-2485

Ridge Road Recreation Center, 800 Ridge Rd., SE (between Burns and Hildreth Streets); (202) 645-3959

Ward 8

Anacostia Fitness Center, 1800 Anacostia Dr., SE (at South Capitol Street); (202) 698-2250

Barry Farm Recreation Center, 1230 Sumner Rd., SE (between MLK Jr. and Firth Sterling Avenues); (202) 645-3896

Douglass Community Center, Frederick Douglass Court and Stanton Terrace, SE; (202) 716-9837

Fort Stanton, 1800 Erie St., SE (between 17th and 18th Streets); (202) 645-5047

Oxon Run, 4th Street and Mississippi Avenue, SE; (202) 645-5042

Arlington (VA) Indoor Pools

Wakefield Pool, 4901 South Chesterfield Rd. (at South Dinwiddle Road); Arlington, VA; (703) 578-3063

Washington-Lee Pool, 1300 North Quincy St. (at 13th Street); Arlington, VA; (703) 228-6262

Yorktown Pool, 5201 North 28th St. (at Yorktown Road); Arlington, VA; (703) 536-9739

Arlington (VA) Recreation Centers

Fitness Centers: $170 for residents/$465 for non-residents
Pools: $242 for residents/$473 for non-residents

Barcroft Sports and Fitness Center, 4200 South Four Mile Run (between South George Mason and Walter Reed Drives); Arlington, VA; (703) 228-0701

Carver Community Center, 1415 South Queen St. (at 13th Road South); Arlington, VA; (703) 228-5706

Fairlington Community Center, 3308 South Stafford St. (between 33rd and 34th Streets); Arlington, VA; (703) 228-6588

Gunston Community Center, 2700 South Lang St. (at 28th Street); Arlington, VA; (703) 228-6980

Langston Brown Community Center & Multipurpose Senior Center, 2121 Culpeper St. (at South Chesterfield Road); Arlington, VA; (703) 228-5210

Madison Community Center, 3829 North Stafford St. (between N. Old Glebe and Military Roads); Arlington, VA; (703) 228-0441

Montgomery County (MD) Indoor Pools
Germantown Indoor Swim Center GISC, 18000 Central Park Circle; Boyds, MD; (240) 777-6830
Martin Luther King, Jr. Swim Center, 1201 Jackson Rd. (off New Hampshire Avenue); Silver Spring, MD; (240) 777-8060
Montgomery Aquatic Center, 5900 Executive Blvd. (at Nicholson Lane); North Bethesda, MD; (240) 777-8070
Olney Indoor Swim Center, 16605 Georgia Ave. (at Emory Lane); Olney, MD; (301) 570-1210

Montgomery County (MD) Outdoor Pools
Bethesda Pool, 6300 Little Falls Pkwy and Hillandale Road; Bethesda, MD; (301) 652-1598
Germantown Outdoor Pool, 18905 Kings View Dr. (at Clopper Road); (240) 777-8067
Long Branch Pool, 8700 Piney Branch Rd. (between University Boulevard E and Flower Avenue); Silver Spring, MD; (240) 777-8066
Martin Luther King Jr. Outdoor Pool, 1201 Jackson Rd. (off New Hampshire Avenue); Silver Spring, MD; (240) 777-8067
Upper County Outdoor Pool, 8201 Emory Grove Rd. (between Woodfield Road and Washington Grove Lane); Gaithersburg, MD; (301) 840-2446
Western County Outdoor Pool, 20151 Fisher Ave. (off Elgin Road); Poolesville, MD; (301) 349-2217
Wheaton/Glenmont Pool, 12621 Dalewood Dr. (at Bluehill Road); Wheaton, MD; (301) 929-5460

Montgomery County (MD) Recreation Centers with Gyms
Fitness Centers: $150 for residents/$165 for non-residents
Pools: $365 for residents/$405 for non-residents
Bauer Drive Community Recreation Center, 14625 Bauer Dr. (at Norbeck Road), Rockville, MD; (301) 468-4015
Clara Barton Neighborhood Recreation Center, 7425 MacArthur Blvd. (at 75th Street); Cabin John, MD; (301) 229-0010
Damascus Community Recreation Center, 25520 Oak Dr. (at Ridge Road); Damascus, MD; (240) 777-6930
East County Community Recreation Center, 3310 Gateshead Manor Way (at Briggs Chaney Road); Silver Spring, MD; (301) 572-7004

Germantown Recreation Center, 18905 Kingsview Rd. (at Clopper Road); Germantown, MD; (301) 601-1680

Gwendolyn E. Coffield Community Recreation Center, 2450 Lyttonsville Rd. (at Lyttonville Place); Silver Spring, MD; (240) 777-4900

Leland Community Recreation Center, 4301 Willow Lane (at 44th Street); Chevy Chase, MD; (301) 652-2249

Long Branch Community Recreation Center, 8700 Piney Branch Rd. (between University Boulevard E and Flower Avenue); Silver Spring, MD; (301) 431-5702

Longwood Community Recreation Center, 19300 Georgia Ave. (off Gold Mine Road); Brookeville, MD; (240) 777-6920

Marilyn J. Praisner Community Recreation Center, 14906 Old Columbia Pike (at Oakhurst Drive); Burtonsville, MD; (240) 777-4970

Potomac Community Recreation Center, 11315 Falls Rd. (at Woodington Drive); Potomac, MD; (240) 777-6960

Ross Boddy Neighborhood Recreation Center, 18529 Brooke Rd. (between Spartan and Chandlee Mill Roads); Sandy Spring, MD; (240) 777-8050

Scotland Neighborhood Recreation Center, 7700 Scotland Dr. (at Seven Locks Road); Potomac, MD; (301) 983-4455

Upper County Neighborhood Recreation Center, 8201 Emory Grove Rd. (between Woodfield Road and Washington Grove Lane); Gaithersburg, MD; (301) 840-2469

Wheaton Neighborhood Recreation Center, 11711 Georgia Ave. (at Hermitage Avenue); Wheaton, MD; (301) 929-5500

Prince George's County (MD) Community Centers

Fitness Center: $110 for residents of Prince George's and Montgomery Counties/$275 for non-residents
Aquatics: $216 for residents/$264 for non-residents

Allentown Fitness & Splash Park, 7210 Allentown Rd. (between Temple Hill Road and Lanhan Road)

Allentown Fitness & Splash Park, Fort Washington, MD; (301) 449-5566 (recorded information), (301) 449-5567 (general inquiries); indoor and outdoor pools and fitness center

Baden Community Center, 13601 Baden-Westwood Rd. (at Baden Naylor Road); Brandywine, MD; (301) 888-1500

Beltsville Community Center, 3900 Sellman Rd. (Little Paint Branch Park); Beltsville, MD; (301) 937-6613

Berwyn Heights Community Center, 6200 Pontiac St. (between 60th and 63rd Avenues); Berwyn Heights, MD; (301) 345-2808

Bladensburg Community Center, 4500 57th Ave. (at 58th Avenue); Bladensburg, MD; (301) 277-2124

Bowie Community Center, SR 450 and Stonybrook Drive; Bowie, MD; (301) 464-1737

Cedar Heights Community Center, 1200 Glen Willow Dr. (Booker T. Homes Park); Seat Pleasant, MD; (301) 773-8881

College Park Community Center, 5051 Pierce Ave. (between 54th and Rhode Island Avenues); College Park, MD; (301) 441-2647

Columbia Park Community Center, 2901 Kent Village Dr. (between Landover and Columbia Park Roads); Landover, MD; (301) 341-3749

Deerfield Run Community Center, 13000 Laurel-Bowie Rd. (between Contee Road and Montpelier Drive); Laurel, MD; (301) 953-7882

Glassmanor Community Center, 1101 Marcy Ave. (Glassmanor Park); Oxon Hill, MD; (301) 567-6033/6034

Glenarden/Theresa Banks Complex, 8615 McLain Ave. (at Irvin Avenue); Glenarden, MD; (301) 772-3151, (301) 772-5516 (pool)

Glenn Dale Community Center, 11901 Glenn Dale Blvd. (at Prospect Hill Road); Glenn Dale, MD; (301) 352-8983

Good Luck Community Center, 8601 Good Luck Rd. (Seabrook Park); Lanham, MD; (301) 552-1093

Harmony Hall Regional Center, 10701 Livingston Rd. (near Fort Washington Road); Fort Washington, MD; (301) 203-6040

Hillcrest Heights Community Center, 2300 Oxon Run Dr. (at 23rd Parkway); Temple Hills, MD; (301) 505-0896

Huntington Community Center, 13022 8th St. (between Maple and Chestnut Avenues); Bowie, MD; (301) 464-3725

Indian Queen Recreation Center, 9551 Fort Foote Rd. (at Round Table Drive); Ft. Washington, MD; (301) 839-9597

John E. Howard Community Center, 4400 Shell St. (Bradbury Heights Park); Capitol Heights, MD; (301) 735-3340

Kentland Community Center, 2411 Pinebrook Ave. (at West Forest Road); Landover, MD; (301) 386-2278

Kettering/Largo Community Center, 431 Watkins Park Dr. (Watkins Regional Park); Upper Marlboro, MD; (301) 390-8390

Lake Arbor Community Center, 10100 Lake Arbor Way (at Campus Way N.); Mitchellville, MD; (301) 333-6561

Langley Park Community Center; 1500 Merrimac Dr. (at 15th Avenue); Hyattsville, MD; (301) 445-4508

Marlow Heights Community Center, 2800 St. Clair Dr. (at 28th Avenue); Marlow Heights, MD; (301) 423-0505

North Brentwood Community Center, 4012 Webster St. (between 40th Street and 41st Avenue); North Brentwood, MD; (301) 864-0756

Oakcrest Community Center, 1300 Capitol Heights Blvd. (Oakcrest Park); Capitol Heights, MD, (301) 736-5355

Palmer Park Community Center, 7720 Barlowe Rd. (at Matthew Henson Avenue), Landover, MD; (301) 773-5665

Patuxent Community Center, 4410 Bishopmill Dr. (at Dario Road); Upper Marlboro, MD; (301) 780-7577

Peppermill Community Center, 610 Hill Rd. (Peppermill Village Park); Landover, MD; (301) 350-8410

Potomac Landing Community Center, 12500 Fort Washington Rd. (at E. Tantallon Road); Fort Washington, MD; (301) 292-9191

Prince George's Plaza Community Center, 6600 Adelphi Rd. (at Beechwood Road); Hyattsville, MD; (301) 864-1611

Rollingcrest-Chillum Community Center, 6120 Sargent Rd. (between Tory Lane and Ray Road); Chillum, MD; (301) 853-2005

Seat Pleasant Activity Center, 5720 Addison Rd. (at Martin Luther King Highway); Seat Pleasant, MD; (301) 773-6685

South Bowie Community Center, 1717 Pittsfield Lane (Amber Meadows Park); Bowie, MD; (301) 249-1622

Stephen Decatur Community Center, 8200 Pinewood Dr. (at Alan Drive); Clinton, MD; (301) 297-4648

Suitland Community Center, 5600 Regency Lane (at Hill Mar Drive); Forestville, MD; (301) 736-3518

Temple Hills Community Center, 5300 Temple Hill Rd. (Temple Hill Park); Temple Hills, MD; (301) 894-6616

Tucker Road Community Center, 1771 Tucker Rd. (Tucker Road Park); Fort Washington, MD; (301) 248-4404

Upper Marlboro Community Center, 5400 Marlboro Race Track Rd. (at Race Track Road); Upper Marlboro, MD; (301) 627-2828

Vansville Community Center, 6813 Ammendale Rd. (at Old Baltimore Pike); Beltsville, MD; (301) 937-6621

Prince George's County (MD) Indoor Pools

Allentown Fitness & Splash Park, 7210 Allentown Rd. (between Temple Hill Road and Lanhan Road); Fort Washington, MD; (301) 449-5566 (recorded information), (301) 449-5567 (general inquiries); indoor and outdoor pools and fitness center

Bickford Natatorium at Prince George's Community College, 301 Largo Rd.; Largo, MD; (301) 322-0979

Fairland Sports and Aquatic Complex, 13820 and 13950 Old Gunpowder Rd. (at Van Dusen Road); Laurel, MD; (301) 362-6060

Prince George's Sports & Learning Complex, 8001 Sheriff Rd. (at Harvey Road); Landover, MD; (301) 583-2400; separate membership required: fitness center, $490 for residents/$580 for non-residents; aquatics, $18 monthly for residents/$22 monthly for non-residents

Theresa Banks Memorial Pool, 8615-A McLain Ave. (at Irvin Avenue); Glenarden, MD; (301) 772-5515, (301) 772-5516

Prince George's County (MD) Outdoor Pools

Summer membership: $54 for residents/$66 for non-residents

Allentown Fitness & Splash Park, 7210 Allentown Rd. (between Temple Hill Road and Lanhan Road); Fort Washington, MD; (301) 449-5566 (recorded information), (301) 449-5567 (general inquiries)

Glenn Dale Splash Park, 11901 Glenn Dale Blvd. (at Prospect Hill Road); Glenn Dale, MD; (301) 352-8983

Hamilton Pool, 3901 Hamilton St. (at 40th Avenue); Hyattsville, MD; (301) 779-8224 (summer), (301) 918-8100 (general inquiries)

J. Franklyn Bourne Memorial Pool, 6500 Calmos St. (between Weston Avenue and Black Dog Street); Seat Pleasant, MD; (301) 350-4422; (301) 918-8100 (general inquiries)

Lane Manor Splash Park, 7601 West Park Dr. (at University Boulevard E); Hyattsville, MD; (301) 422-7284, (301) 918-8100 (general inquiries)

North Barnaby Pool, 5000 Wheeler Rd. (at Iverson Place), Oxon Hill, MD; (301) 894-1150, (301) 449-5566

Rollingcrest-Chillum Splash Pool, 6122 Sargent Rd. (between Tory Place and Ray Road); Chillum, MD; (301) 853-9115

INDEX

ABOUT THE AUTHOR

Rob Grader is a writer, producer, actor, and proud cheap bastard living outside Washington, D.C. He created the Cheap Bastard's Guidebook series; his other writing credits include *The Cheap Bastard's Guide to New York City* (Globe Pequot Press, 2008) and *The Cuddle Sutra* (Source Books, 2007). He has also written for *Time Out New York, AM New York,* and the *Guardian*. Rob received the Lowell Thomas Award for the Best Guidebook of the Year. He also created and produced the A&E reality series *House of Dreams*. A graduate of the American Repertory Theater's Institute at Harvard University, Grader has appeared at regional theaters around the country and on *Law & Order, Law & Order: SVU,* and *The Job,* and in the film *American Splendor*; www.thecheapbastard.com.